THE LAST SHALL BE FIRST

THE LAST
SHALL BE FIRST

*THE COLOURFUL STORY OF
JOHN LOBB
THE ST. JAMES'S BOOTMAKERS*

BY

BRIAN DOBBS

ELM TREE BOOKS
HAMISH HAMILTON · LONDON

First published in Great Britain 1972
by Elm Tree Books
90 Great Russell Street London WC1

Copyright © 1972 Brian Dobbs

SBN 241 02273 8

Printed in Great Britain
Northumberland Press Ltd, Gateshead

Contents

Acknowledgements		xi
1.	'The Last Luxury of Noble Minds'	1
2.	The Making of the Shoe	7
3.	The Ancient Craft	14
4.	Limping to London	25
5.	There's Gold in Them Thar Heels	33
6.	Fame ... by Appointment	42
7.	Awards and 'Pussentidges'	51
8.	Family Matters	62
9.	Boots for Bosie	69
10.	War and Profits	83
11.	Kings and Uncommoners	93
12.	Celebrities and Slumps	100
13.	Bootmaker by Accident	109
14.	Lest We Forget	117
15.	American Hospitality	128
16.	Plus Ça Change	137
	Index	143

DEDICATED AT MR. ERIC LOBB'S
SPECIAL REQUEST TO
LIGHT

In June 1971, Eric Lobb wrote to congratulate H.R.H. the Duke of Edinburgh on his fiftieth birthday. The Duke's reply is reproduced below (with the kind permission of His Royal Highness):

Dear Mr. Lobb,

Thank you very much for your good wishes.
One of the reasons I am going so well must be that
I have always been well shod.

yours sincerely

Philip

ACKNOWLEDGEMENTS

The author and the publishers wish to express their gratitude to John Murray, Publishers, and to Sir Philip Magnus for permission to reproduce on page 46 the extract from Sir Philip's biography of King Edward VII.

The author also wishes to thank Mr. Eric Lobb and his staff for unfailing courtesy and co-operation in long conversations and interviews about the affairs of the Lobb family and firm, and for making available documents and records, some of a private and confidential nature.

I

'THE LAST LUXURY OF NOBLE MINDS'

A FAVOURITE joke in the boot and shoe industry is the story
of the man who takes his shoes in for repair in September
1939. He leaves the shoes, war breaks out and he is called up.
Six years later, on his demob, he finds the repair ticket in his
wallet and remembering his shoes, finds his way to a bomb-
damaged street which has one premises still standing—the
shoemaker's. He goes in and hands over the ticket. Con-
sternation. Frantic search of premises takes place. Eventually, a pair of shoes with six years' accumulation of dust is
brought up from the cellar.
'Would these be them, sir?'
'Yes, that's them.'
'Good, They'll be ready next Tuesday!'
The story may be authentic, but it certainly would not
have taken place at John Lobb's, the bootmakers of St
James's London. There, one feels, as a gleaming pair appears
as if by magic, the poker-faced answer would be 'Here you
are, sir. What kept you?'
To step into the Lobb premises in St James's Street is to
be aware immediately that this is no ordinary run-of-the-mill
shop. Not that the façade should fool you. Its polished
wood door and windows are of strictly modern vintage, yet
its discreet appearance is redolent of a previous age, a
cunning piece of artifice rather than genuine antiquity. But
then, who would want a bootmaker's to look like a supermarket? And, once inside, the appearance and atmosphere

should satisfy anyone hungry for a nostalgic glimpse of older, more leisurely and elegant times.

On one side stands a Lobb museum of shoemaker's tools: two large show-cases of boots, shoes and lasts (Queen Victoria's included), a case of shining silver spurs, a display case of gold and silver medals awarded to the firm, and a Royal warrant from the King of Thailand which reads, in translation,

The Royal Thai Embassy
21 Ashburn Place
London SW7
Bureau of the Royal Household

This letter of appointment is issued to Mr Eric John Lobb, of London, in order to certify that the President of the Council of Ministers has received the Royal Command to appoint Mr Eric John Lobb as the Royal Bootmaker to his majesty the King as from now on,

May you be blessed with continued prosperity.

12th July, Buddhist Era 2504 (1961)
(AD) Field Marshal S. Dhanarajata
Affixed with the Official Seal

If the visitor looks back after his first tentative steps along the patterned red carpet, he will see a large photograph above him of King Edward VII, first of the firm's many Royal patrons, its stationary eyes unnervingly following him around the premises. More likely, however, is that he will see first the portrait in oils of the original John Lobb which hangs at the back of the shop. Again, a formidable pair of eyes weighs in the balance whether the newcomer is likely to prove a worthy recipient of a pair of Lobb shoes. Noel Barber once wittily suggested that Lobb's of London is where the shoes choose you, and the founder, if the painter has done him justice, looks as if he heartily approves that interpretation of the coming proceedings.

Before our visitor can scrutinise the mounted certificates and awards from a host of bygone international exhibitions, or read Eric Lobb's warrants as Royal Bootmaker to both Her Majesty Queen Elizabeth II and His Royal Highness the Duke of Edinburgh, or examine the documents that proclaim the firm 'Boot and Shoe Makers to His Imperial Majesty the Shahanshah Aryamehr of Iran' and 'Bootmaker to the August Sovereign, His Imperial Majesty the Emperor of Ethiopia', a polite cough or a discreet greeting will make him aware that an apron-fronted or overalled attendant is ready to do his bidding. Unless he exudes credit-worthiness from every pore, or his face is instantly recognisable, he will be quietly asked from whom his introduction to the world of Lobb comes.

One is irresistibly reminded, not of a shop, but of a private club, where the name of a valued present member is the best passport of all. To pursue the analogy, these are premises where those of like mind meet and discuss their common problems: in this case, their feet. One may go to, say, Lilley and Skinner's and buy a pair of shoes; if anyone claimed to have gone to Lobb's to have his nethermost extremities satis-factorily caparisoned, the term would perhaps be more fitting to the deed.

The preliminaries completed, our visitor will be eased into a leather-backed armchair and his feet will be measured by a fitter with loving care, every distinctive feature, to the smallest bunion, carefully catalogued, and then outlines of each foot traced meticulously in the last-maker's pattern book. From this vital information, his new shoes will be constructed to accommodate every individual idiosyncrasy. He may not receive them for months, but when he does he will receive a pair of shoes or boots that are uniquely and supremely his and his alone. He will pay a high price for the privilege, but by setting the fee against the services of highly trained and skilful craftsmen, and against the guarantee of a pheno-menally long life for his shoes, the high investment can be made to look modest indeed. Also, at any time in the future, another pair can be made for him which will be identical in measurement in every way. So long as there are people like him with the money to spend, Lobb's will flourish.

So, leaving behind a record as telling as his fingerprints, our visitor steps back into the street, the all-pervasive and lingering smell of leather still in his nostrils, and, if there is anything of a Walter Mitty quality in his soul, hailing not a taxi but a hansom cab to take him to his club.

That there is a quality of romance inherent in such an experience is upheld by documentary evidence such as the following.

In 1956, the *Daily Mail* sent the veteran novelist Charles Morgan to see the 83-year-old Max Beerbohm lying gravely ill in a clinic in Rapallo, Italy. The distinguished essayist, caricaturist and critic had in his long life seen more of the elegant high life than most, and one would think his association with such men as George Moore, Oscar Wilde and Bernard Shaw in his youth, and his later elevation to the Grand Old Man of English Letters, would have placed him far above such prosaic matters as shoes. The great Max's opening remark to Morgan was not about the theatre or about London society or any of the hundred topics one might have expected. It was, simply 'Tell me, is Lobb still the best bootmaker in London?'

And what of the American magazine *Esquire*? They have thrived for years on the effective formula of feeding their readers dreams of joining high society, and proffering advice on the accoutrements of dress necessary to make débutantes go weak at the knees and society hostesses clamour for a visit. To *Esquire*, one of the secrets to figuring on those best-dressed men lists was to have the money to afford the 'invaluable collaboration' of bootmakers 'like Lobb of St James's Street in London'. They added, perhaps in case their readers were relatively unlikely to hop on a plane without a bonus at the other end, that the St James's Street establishment was 'one of the most beautiful shops in the world'.

When it was necessary in a Sexton Blake story, *The Mystery of Avenue Road*, to introduce a superior Scotland

Yard officer, author Anthony Parsons made him a model of
sartorial elegance:

The Yard ace was in all his glory—check suit, grey homburg,
gleaming Lobb shoes, yellow malacca stick and yellow gloves all
complete.
  'And a gun in my back pocket!' he announced, when Blake
pretended to shield his eyes from the shining glory of the man.

On a loftier literary plane, a character in Robert Speaight's
The Angel in the Mist makes a far-reaching claim:

'Beautiful brogues these,' he said suddenly, pointing to his feet 'Lobb
of course, Lobb and Lock (the hatters) are the two last luxuries
of noble minds ...'

And when Sir Philip Gibbs was proving the unique qualities
of John Galsworthy ('nobility is rare among those who write
books ...' he snobbishly proclaimed), he marshalled in
evidence not *The Forsyte Saga* but the fact that Galsworthy
'bought his boots at Lobb's'.
  Against fierce competition from industrialised competitors
at home and abroad, which sent countless numbers of
similar firms to the wailing walls of Carey Street, Lobb's
have (no pun intended) lasted. How close they came to an
ignominious end, and how delicately poised on the razor's
edge of ultimate disaster they have sometimes been, will
emerge in these pages. But for the grace of some benevolent
deity, and by some uncanny freaks of timing, Lobb's would
be lost in oblivion with the rest of the hand-made bootmakers who once flourished all over the West End of
London; and this book would never have been written.
Theirs is not only the story of the craft, it is also the story of
a family; the two are inseparable and equally fascinating.
  To begin to understand how they succeeded, it is necessary
to go back to the life of the founder, the original John Lobb,
sitter for the portrait which not altogether benignly gazes
down on the comings and goings at the present day pre-

mises; to go back, more precisely, to Christmas 1829 and a tiny Cornwall cottage; but first it may well be advisable to examine the craft of bootmaking and the history of the industry to put his life in its true perspective.

2

THE MAKING OF THE SHOE

AT ABOUT the same time as our visitor to Lobb's stepped out on to the street, his vital statistics, or at least his foot's vital statistics, had been handed on to the last-maker. This worthy gentleman works not with pliable leather, but with hard blocks of wood. Taking a firm, well-grained block of maple, beech or hornbeam, the last-maker transforms the timber into a smoothly contoured model of the foot itself.

This translation of abstract outlines and basic measurements into a three dimensional model is as exacting and, one suspects, as inwardly rewarding as a wood carving by Barbara Hepworth or Henry Moore. Roughing out the shape with a special knife, looking for all the world like a boy scout whittling away with his pen knife, the last-maker gets to an approximation of the desired shape and size, then brings all his skill to bear with rasp and sandpaper to reconstruct an exact model of the individual foot.

Anyone who has ever tried to sculpt will know the difference between modelling, where one builds gradually to a desired shape with a pliable material, and the infinitely more difficult process of carving where there can be no errors and what has been cut away cannot be replaced. Part of the last-maker's rare skill is the ability to 'see' a shape in his mind and release it from its wooden surroundings. Surprisingly enough, there are any number of possible shapes which will conform to the original measurements, and every last-maker prides himself on being able to create a particular kind of shape which conforms to the measurements. This ensures not only that the shoe will eventually fit the foot perfectly, but also that it will legitimately impart an appearance of elegance and style. It is possible to talk of 'ugly' lasts, and of 'beautiful' lasts. The beauty of the typical Lobb last with a stylish toe is one of the secrets of the firm's success. They are, however, realistic enough to admit that if fashions changed radically they would be perfectly prepared to change their lasts. 'We'd put the heel on the toe if that's what the customer wants and pays for!'

In the St James's Street premises, there are racks and racks of lasts, replicas to the last corn and contusion of over twenty thousand pairs of feet; each pair labelled with the customer's name, and looking as if some ghostly wooden army has encamped for the night then departed hurriedly in the morning, leaving, in their haste, all their wooden boots behind them. To Lobb's, it is a filing system and library rolled into one.

From the last-maker we now turn to another expert craftsman in his own right, the 'clicker' or cutter-out. Clickers claim for themselves the honorary title of the aristocrats of the trade, although other craftsmen may dispute the claim. Clicking is a vaguely comic term which recurs in another ancient trade, that of printing. Presumably derived from the Dutch *klikken* or the French *cliquer*, the term 'clicker' denotes the foreman shoemaker who cuts out the leather and distributes the work (in printing, the clicker distributes copy to the compositors), rather than describing any vocal effects he may make while carrying out his tasks.

To anyone but a clicker or a leatherworker, a piece of leather is a piece of leather is a piece of leather, as Gertrude Stein might have said. To one of those gentlemen, such a thought would be blasphemy. To them, each and every skin or hide has individual characteristics and is worthy of the respect one normally affords to an individual. Its weight, its pliability, its grain, its colour is carefully assessed and, guided by his long experience, the clicker will cut out the pieces (at least eight separate pieces for one shoe) which will eventually form the upper part of the shoe.

Taking such esoteric factors as the weight and individuality of the eventual wearer into account, he cuts the pieces out with a knife so sharp he could also shave with it if he so desired. I have yet to see anyone actually shave with a clicker's knife, but there is no doubt about its efficacy for cutting up sandwiches.

The skins and hides themselves vary according to the kind of shoe required. In the highest class work, Russia Calf will be used for brown shoes and Waxed Calf for black shoes. There is also Brown Grain Calf, Antelope, Doe-skin, and the quaintly named Ooze or Reverse Calf (all of them for brown shoes); and Box Calf, Grain Hide, or Patent for black shoes. Less frequently used are Willow Calf and Scotch Grain (both brown), and Crup and Beva (both black).

If those all seem relatively prosaic, one can always choose some other representative of the animal kingdom, say crocodile, lizard, elephant, rhino, ostrich, seal-skin or kangaroo. The experienced clicker will undoubtedly take it all in his stride.

Incidentally, these are all upper leathers and, at Lobb's at least the soles will usually be an English tanned Oak-Bark, solid, stolid and long-wearing.

When the work of the last-maker and the clicker is completed, the closer takes over. As his title suggests, he is responsible for the final construction of the upper, and however good the last-making or the clicking, he can ruin the appearance of the shoe if his contribution is not up to standard. He has already cut paper patterns of every piece of leather to be used and he trims the leather pieces to their final shapes, knowing from the last what form they should take. He then sews all the pieces together, incorporating any stiffeners or linings, and fitting them precisely to the last.

When the upper is thus completed it goes, on its last, to the maker. The maker now adds the sole and heel, and needs every bit of craftsmanship he can muster. This final union of sole and upper is an exacting job that can take two days or more. The inner sole leather will have been soaked overnight in water to make it 'mellow' and is then moulded to the bottom of the last while the upper is drawn taut and sewn to the welt. The tensions have to be even throughout the shoe until the upper fits like a cosy glove around the top of the last, without slackness or undue pressure anywhere.

Then, our maker stitches the sole to the welt, operating on a precise number of stitches to the inch relative to the weight of the leather and the shoe. Later he adds the heel which is built up piece by piece with rivets. (The extra-ordinary amount of material which makes up the bottom of the shoe—the welt, the stiffeners, the lifting for heels, the inner and outer soles, the lining and a layer of tarry felt to eliminate 'squeaks'—has been selected and trimmed by the rough-stuff cutter, another highly trained craftsman.) The shoe has been made, and the maker completes his triumph with the first polish.

Fitter, last-maker, clicker, closer, rough-stuff cutter and maker will have all served a five-year apprenticeship, after which they will increase their knowledge and experience perhaps for fifty years. The man who now takes over the shoe serves no apprenticeship but, in his way, is as skilled as his colleagues. This is the polisher. He brings the shoes to their final pristine glory. Using brushes, cloths, fingers, thumbs, polish, water and, if the management are not around, spit, the shoes are brought to a deep, satisfying, glowing finish. Many customers will expect to wait for months *after* the shoes are constructed until they have been polished and polished and polished.

The Waxed Calf listed among the available skins is, for the polisher, a special challenge. For a novice to attempt to shine it normally results in an unholy mess. This is because, unlike most leathers, it has not the hair side outwards but the flesh side. As one would expect, it was much more commonly used in the days when every gentleman could call on a few hours of his valet's time to get his shoes or boots polished. It has to be done, not with brush and polish, but with liquid blacking and a bone. A deer bone is used to stroke the leather gently to make it smooth and supple, then the blacking is added, and then the bone is used again until a perfect finish is assured.

So, by the uncanny skill of six craftsmen, another pair of Lobb boots or shoes is born. It may have taken a year, although four months is average. Meanwhile, in factories in Northampton and elsewhere, machines have been churning out toecaps at a rate of thousands in a minute, or stitching soles to uppers before an operator can blink.

In, for example, the 1930s, in an up-to-date factory, an ordinary shoe would have been operated on by about 80 people, each responsible for some small task. The shoe would bring perhaps 150 different machines into use, performing somewhere between 200 and 500 operations. Even earlier, in 1914-1918, under the pressure of the demands of war, Northampton had made 23 million pairs of boots for the British army.

However, even if a machine were developed to wear the shoes for you, it would never match the accumulated and inherited skill and craftsmanship that has gone into that one pair of Lobb shoes, tailored to its future owner's individual requirement as carefully as if it were a suit of clothes. It is in return for that sort of skill and service, that an ever increasing number of people are prepared to pay fifty guineas and upwards for a pair of Lobb shoes and eschew the factory product at five or six guineas.

Lobb's patrons are indeed discriminating customers, and they expect a service to justify the price paid. Requests for Lobb laces to be sent 5,000 miles are a common occurrence. The East Indian gentleman with his magnifying glass and the guards officer who tries to tear his shoes apart are not exceptional. Lobb's can also tell of the engineer who used to send full blueprints of the shoes he wanted and was prepared to allow no more tolerance than one sixty-fourth of an inch in the making, and of the London man-about-town who places his new Lobb shoes on the carpet and lies on his stomach to inspect them from grasshopper level. One customer, staying in a suite at Claridge's, phoned for a skilled Lobb craftsman to taxi over to his hotel to fit, not a new pair of shoes, but a new pair of laces. (The craftsman obliged, of course.)

It is for these and equally discriminating, if less eccentric, patrons, that Lobb's have stayed in business. Survival has depended very largely upon the superiority of the hand-made article to the cheap and instantly available machine product.

Lobb's began their operations at a time when hand-sewn boots were well-nigh universal and the factory system, in this particular industry at least, was in a rudimentary stage. Boots were made predominantly not on large premises but by small-scale master bootmakers who lived and worked at home. The fascinating point about Lobb's is that this is precisely the system which they, almost alone, have perpetuated. The ten or so craftsmen one sees in the St James's Street premises working in full view of the customers (which has its own fascination for a visitor) represent the tip of the iceberg.

In small backrooms and workshops in their own homes, whether in London, Newcastle, Bristol, Exeter, Glasgow or elsewhere, many craftsmen work for Lobb's without ever setting foot in St James's Street. The work is sent to them and once completed is sent back to headquarters for the eventual customers. So, a pair of shoes for the Emperor of Abyssinia may, at this moment, be being made in a small room in Glasgow. If they are, one can be sure that the Glasgow craftsman will, without ever being in the royal presence, know more about His Serene Highness's feet than the Emperor does himself.

To return to the middle of the nineteenth century, when the firm started, is to see not how great, but how small the changes in the intervening period have been. A look at

Lobb's even today is to look at history, and to see not only a surviving, but a flourishing representative of methods and attitudes which time has swept away in so many fields. As the family grocer disappears before the onslaught of the supermarket chains, and the hand-carved article goes down before the moulded plastic, Lobb's, almost alone, continue to grow. To do justice to their achievement, I now give some indication of the background of the craft's history.

3

THE ANCIENT CRAFT

THE CRAFT of shoe-making has existed ever since one of our anonymous ancestors hit upon the brilliantly simple idea of covering his foot. Like all the best inventions from the wheel to the egg-cup, it caught on. And as long as there were feet, there was a demand for shoemakers.

A British Museum painting, taken from a wall of Thebes and dating roughly from the Exodus, shows two shoe-makers making sandals—one of them using a clicking knife strikingly similar to today's article. By 1495 B.C. therefore, shoemakers were in business and indeed there are a number of Biblical and other references to confirm this. In the Apocrypha, Judith's sandals 'ravished' the eyes of Holofernes, but did him little good for she then slew him. 'Your shoes on your feet' was a necessary supplement to girding up your loins, according to *Exodus*, and both that common expression 'I wouldn't mind being in your shoes', and the traditional ceremony of sending off a bride and groom with an old shoe in tow, stem from a custom under Mosaic Law of taking off shoes and presenting them to others as a token of goodwill.

The body of literature associated with the craft is very small, and in the British Museum the ravages of war were particularly severe on this part of the book collection. That which does exist tends to describe shoemakers and their associates as exponents of the 'gentle craft'. We read of St Crispin, the patron saint of shoemakers. St Crispin was born about A.D. 303 at Rome, and fell under the régime of

Galerius, one of the many Roman Emperors to persecute Christians. Because Crispin made as many converts for Christianity as shoes for their feet, he was duly martyred.

St Hugh was believed to have bequeathed his bones to the shoemakers to make them into tools in return for their kindness during his lifetime. By the sixteenth century, there is a play called *George-a-Green* which refers to Edward IV toasting a band of shoemakers in these terms:

> Marry, because you have drunk with the King,
> And the King has so graciously pledged you,
> You shall no more be called shoe-makers,
> But you and yours to the world's end
> Shall be called the trade of the gentle craft.

By the eighteenth century, there are references to such worthy representatives of this 'gentle craft' as William Carey, the Northamptonshire philanthropist, who, having served as an apprentice at 14, is his own master at 19, but left it all to become a preacher and a missionary to India; and to Robert Bloomfield of Suffolk, apprenticed at 11, and better known for pastoral poems like 'The Farmer's Boy'; and to William Gifford, who worked out algebraic problems and pious verses with a blunt awl on leather during his long apprenticeship to an unsympathetic master, went to Oxford and eventually founded the *London Quarterly Review*. Even earlier, in the seventeenth century, lived George Fox, another apprentice who became deeply religious and is remembered today as the founder of the Society of Friends.

Now one can see why such estimable men feature so largely in the history of their 'gentle craft'. No public relations officer for the industry could do much better in finding men to show the craft in a good light. (Historians of the shoe industry tend to choose titles like *The Romance of the Shoe* and *Once Upon a Time*.)

This is not just a British phenomenon either. In Germany, attention is always drawn to the philosopher-cobbler Hans

Sachs, a real life Mastersinger who lived in Nuremburg
from 1494 to 1576, author of some six thousand poems. One
needs no knowledge of German to get the gist of the lines:

> Hans Sachs war ein Schuh—
> Macher und Poet dazu.

and when Wagner made Sachs the subject of his happiest
creation, *Die Meistersinger von Nurnberg*, the score of
which, by the way, includes a chorus in honour of St Crispin,
the immortality of Hans Sachs was assured.

When one also considers such epic and complimentary
lines as,

> The Crispin Trade! What better trade can be?
> Ancient and famous, independent, free!
> No other trade a brighter claim can find,
> No other trade displays more wealth of mind!
> No other calling prouder names can boast,
> In arms, in arts—themselves a perfect host!
> All honour, zeal and patriotic pride;
> To dare heroic and in suffering tried!

clearly the wholesale canonisation of clickers, closers,
makers *et al* to join their saintly Crispin in some glorious
Valhalla of the Last cannot be long delayed.

But this may not be so accurate a picture of the shoemakers of the past. By digging a little deeper and looking
afresh at the evidence, the overwhelming impression is very
different indeed. In fact, one might go so far as to say that
shoemakers have been as independently-minded, as radical,
as intractable and as bloody-minded as any comparable band
of workers in any other industry. And good luck to
them.

It does them a disservice to pretend, or to get the impression, that nobility goes along with the awl, the bristle,
the thread and the polish. Theirs has been the strength of
mind and the independence of spirit of the true craftsman
who makes his own conditions, demands a just price for his

labours, eschews a journey into a factory when he can work without supervision at home, and treats with his employer not with the artificial strength of combination, but with the real strength of a man who has invested a lifetime's labour in his craft and knows that his is a rare and special gift.

These are not the men to tug the forelock; and, to impart another Lobb trade secret, it is the fostering over the years of a satisfactory relationship between Lobb's and the men, and the men and Lobb's that has formed a two-way loyalty. Depending upon which way you look at it, it is a fair job for a fair pay, or a fair pay for a fair job. One Lobb outworker, Billy Bower, came to Lobb's for a job in 1892 and held it for over sixty years without ever visiting the premises again —and he only lived a fourpenny bus ride away.

I cannot think that the true antecedents of a Billy Bower, are the George Foxes and the Hans Sachs of the world. One has to turn to a different sort of tradition and one, I am sure, much nearer to reality. One of the first to give us a convincing picture of a shoemaker, was the Elizabethan playwright Thomas Dekker.

Little is known about Dekker. He was born in London about 1570 and died some time between the years 1632 and 1640, and he certainly spent at least seven years in a debtors' prison. His fame rests securely on the robust, exuberant and intimate pictures of the London life of his day, and particularly on his masterpiece, *The Shoemaker's Holiday*, alternatively titled *The Gentle Craft*.

At his hands, the secondary title looks ironic. The play is about Simon Eyre, a shoemaker who becomes Lord Mayor of London (in fact, the original Simon Eyre was a master draper who became Mayor in 1445, but must have been a rather naïve youth for he is supposed to have served a seven-year apprenticeship to an upholsterer in the firm belief that his master was a draper, and only transferred to another master at the end of the seven years). Eyre, his foreman Hodge, his journeymen Ralph and Firk, and a maid, Cicely Bumtrinket (Dekker making many a *double entendre* on the last two names) are very happy creations, full of life and vigour and entertaining throughout the duration of the play.

Firk asks, '... have you all your tools, a good rubbing-pin, a good stopper, a good dresser, your four sorts of awls, and your two balls of wax, your paring knife, your hand and thumb leathers, and good St Hugh's bones to smooth up your work?'

So clearly not much in the way of tools has changed in the course of 270 years.

His master, Simon Eyre, is well aware of his importance as a shoemaker: 'Am I not Simon Eyre? Are not these my brave men, my brave shoemakers, all gentlemen of the Gentle Craft? Prince am I none, yet I am nobly born, as being the sole son of a shoemaker ...'

But for a self-styled prince and gentleman, he has a fine line in invective. When his staff have forgotten to clean out his shop, they are 'fat mid-riff, swag-belly whores' and 'powder-beef queans', but the interesting thing is that his journeymen give as good as they get. When he tells Firk to wash his face, Firk's rejoinder is 'Let them wash my face that will eat it ...'

Equally, however much Eyre may curse them, he is insistent that his workmen should only tackle high-class work: 'Fie, defile not thy fine workmanlike fingers with the feet of kitchen-stuff and basting-ladles. Ladies of the court, fine ladies, my lads, commit their feet to our apparelling ... Yark [*i.e.* stitch tightly] and seam, yark and seam!'

Over the next few centuries it is the sturdy independence of a Simon Eyre or a Firk which continually asserts itself. An analysis of the crowd who played such a momentous role in the French revolution shows an astonishing number of shoemakers among them. In London life in the eighteenth century, who were notorious for drunkenness and disorder? None but the shoemakers! From whose ranks did many radical agitators and protestors of the early nineteenth century arise? From none other than that happy band of men—the shoemakers!

Thomas Hardy, first secretary of the London Corresponding Society formed in 1792 to strive for Parliamentary reform, and tried for high treason for his efforts in the cause, was a shoemaker. Charles Pendrill, tried as a leading conspirator with the notorious Colonel Despard who had served with Nelson and was seized in 1802 for organising an underground army, was a journeyman shoemaker. So was Allan Davenport who led a successful strike in the trade in 1813 which forced a detailed price-list upon the masters; and so was Thomas Preston, who was an active and prominent organiser of the Spa Fields demonstration of 1816, a demonstration directed against the misery and post-war unemployment of the period that had 45,000 people out of work in Spitalfields alone.

Knowing of such men, it comes as no surprise to learn that of the members of the Cato Street conspiracy of 1820, a band who plotted an unconvincing scheme to assassinate the entire cabinet of the day, the majority were boot and shoemakers. The conspiracy was an abortive venture which cost five men their lives on the gallows, and five their livelihoods when they were transported.

Later in the century, it was the home of the shoe industry in Northampton which returned the atheist Charles Bradlaugh to the House of Commons time and again after the Commons had rejected him.

Writing in 1850, the journalist Henry Mayhew, famous for his accounts of the London underworld and the London poor, may have found the reason why the so-called 'gentle craft' on so many occasions has acted ignobly. He thought shoemakers '... certainly far from an unintellectual body of men. They appear to be a stern, uncompromising and reflecting race. This, perhaps, is to be accounted for by the solitude of their employment developing their own internal resources, and producing that particular form of mental temperament which is generally accompanied with austerity

of manner ... the shoemakers are distinguished for the
severity of their manners and habits of thought, and the
suspicion that seems to pervade their character ...'

I will return to Mayhew in a moment, but, on a lighter
note, could there be a better example of independence and
resourcefulness than the case of the Frenchman Monsieur
Matthieu who had to appear at the Bar of the Paris Tribunal
in January 1860? He had long been harassed for money in
his small Parisian shoemaking business, particularly by
customers who took the product but took a long time to
pay him. He came up with what would seem to have been
a brilliant idea. He circularised his customers with an
announcement that he was about to write and publish his
memoirs, an important section of which would be devoted
to biographies of his customers' feet. These would read
something like: Madame de —— of Rue ——, Number
——. Married 1840, has three children, pays badly if at all,
feet very difficult to fit, flattened arches, two bunions, four
corns, walks awkwardly and wears her shoes out on the
inside because she is knock-kneed.

All his customers had to do to avoid his breach of professional etiquette, was to send him fifteen francs to be
excluded from the book! Regrettably, the idea brought
him a month's term of imprisonment, instead of his
desperately needed francs.

But to return to Mayhew. The evidence relating to the
state of the industry at the time that the original John Lobb
set up in the trade is relatively meagre. Fortunately, Mayhew, who did so much to bring public attention to the
miseries and working conditions of the ordinary labourer
that lay behind the façade of Victorian metropolitan prosperity, did once turn his attention to the shoe trade. In a
series of articles in the form of letters which appeared under
the bland anonymity of 'Our Correspondent', the *Morning
Post* covered a number of metropolitan trades and pro-
fessions. Some of the letters, each 10,000 words long, are
about boot and shoemakers.

John Lobb,
founder of the firm

The founder's son,
William Hunter Lobb, Edwardian
businessman

His grandson,
the late William Lobb

William's brother, Eric Lobb,
the present proprietor

The Cornish cottage that John Lobb left to walk to London

The Lobb family on the steps of their home at Alexandra Road, St John's Wood, in the summer of 1908. Betsy Lobb stands at the head of the group, a floral-hatted nanny holds baby Eric, while two parlourmaids stand guard over his two brothers William (*left*) and Victor

The first surprising thing to be learned is that in London, apart from domestic servants, of whom there were 168,701, and general labourers in various trades who totalled 50,279, there were more boot and shoemakers than any other. There was a colossal 28,574, making it easily the largest handicraft, and the third most popular occupation of all. Considering that there were only about 20,000 clerks and about 6,500 bricklayers, the craft assumes an importance which makes it altogether surprising that it has received so little attention from economic historians.

Mayhew's figures come from 1841 sources and may not be totally reliable, but they are certainly indicative of general trends. By using the Post Office Directory, Mayhew then calculated that just over 2,000 of the total 28,574 were master bootmakers and giving employment to the remaining 26,000.

Clearly, whoever wished to join this trade as an outsider could be sure of some stiff competition. As Mayhew makes clear, part of the trouble was that the numbers in the industry had increased phenomenally: against an increase of about 10 per cent in the population of the country from 1831 to 1841, the numbers in the shoe trade had increased by about 30 per cent. The inevitable result of this influx was that wages declined, and this trend continued from 1830 to 1850. Mayhew calculated that an average wage in 1840 was about 15s 2¾d a week. By 1850, it was 12s 1¾d. There are too many variables and external influences to rely wholly on these figures, but it certainly appears that all was not well.

Mayhew talked to workmen, employers, union organisers and so on. He makes clear differentiation between the East End of London and the West End. In the East, the dismal picture of sweat shops, exploitation, disgraceful working conditions, shoddy materials and careless workmanship speaks volumes. In the West End, there was more respect for the craft itself; it was clearly recognised that closing and making were two separate and specialised processes giving employment to two highly skilled men (a differentiation which was apparently 'rigorously maintained in London more than elsewhere').

The lot of the worker in the higher-class trade of London's West End was a good deal less severe than that of his counterpart in the East, but that should not give the impression that life was a bed of roses. The boots were by all accounts superb pieces of craftsmanship, but a great deal of human misery and toil under trying circumstances went into their construction. Mayhew gives the testimony of a man he calls 'an intelligent member of the West End trade', who gives an eloquent picture of life in the trade in 1850.

I am a boot-closer, working for the best shop, I am not fully employed. I have an equal share of work with my shop-mates, and try to fill up my spare time with what we call 'by-strokes' (that is by seeking for extra employment at other shops). I get the best prices. In the course of last season I have made, with an apprentice and my wife's assistance, and working Sunday and all the rest of the week, and sitting up for two entire nights in the course of that time—with this I have made, I say, as much as £3. How much I earned of that sum I cannot say—I might have done half of it. I think I could earn 35s for one week at a time in the season, but then I couldn't keep it up at that rate. I can myself, without any assistance, earn with comfort 27s a week when I can get it. To do that much, however, I must sit at my work for 14 hours every day. Out of the 27s I shall have to pay about 1s 6d for grindery, and 9d for oil for my light. So that my clear week's earnings would be between 24s and 25s. When I was a single man my average earnings throughout the year came to £1 2s 6d per week, but I had a good seat of work all that time. I think my average wages during that time were, in the season (that is from April to July), about 26s a week, and out of season about £1 a week. Single-handed I think I earn about the same now.

A great number of closers earn less than I do; some may earn a bit more. I think that, to take the average of the closers generally, throughout the town, their income would be about a £1 a week. In some individual instances the weekly earnings might be as low as 15s; but I know that the accounts taken of the earning of the whole trade, in and out of union, in 1837, gave an average of 17s a week to each of the 13,000 individuals who then followed the business in London. Since that time wages have gone down about 15 per cent. At this rate, I calculate the average wages of our body would be about 15s per man ... But the hands generally have less to do than they had in 1838, owing to the greater number of people working at the trade. I should say ... each man has 10 per cent less work to do; so that I calculate ... an average ... now ... should be 13s 6d a week each.

In 1812 the bootmakers received their highest wages. If an average could have been taken then of the earnings of the trade [it would have been about] 35s per man ... I know myself that my late master used to earn £2 per week on an average many years back, but of late years I am sure he has not made 15s a week.

He goes on to outline the causes of the decline: the importation of French boots and shoes from a country where rents and wages were much lower (as the man had himself worked in France for a spell he evidently knew what he was talking about, and if we remember that Peel's tariff reforms of 1842 had slashed the price of men's boots by as much as 2s 6d a pair, this has the ring of truth); the increase of competition from the growing factories of Northampton (where it was said 'every child ... has a leather apron'); and the ruthless price war not only between master and master, but also between worker and worker, in cutting prices and costs to withstand the French and Northampton competition (in other words there were more people each fighting for a larger slice of a smaller cake).

One of Lobb's present workers, Jim Saunders, is from a family whose craftsmanship has been handed down from generation to generation as a living tradition; he told me how his grandfather used to work in the 1850s, when the only possible way to continue with the exacting fine stitching after daylight hours was by candlelight. Grandfather Saunders made his own candles from tallow wax with a thread for a wick. By placing a bottle of water between the work, which he held on his knees, and the candle, he was able to focus the maximum light on what he was doing. When one remembers the difficulties of doing much less exacting tasks by the flickering light of candles during the recent power cuts, one can only marvel at the skill and perseverance of such men. It was the only thing that kept them from starving, as Mayhew's witness has shown.

This was the stage on which our first protagonist, the original John Lobb, was to step, and on which he could have found triumph or disaster. If he had been just an ordinary man, or even just an ordinary bootmaker, his name would not have lived on, but then John Lobb was anything but ordinary.

4

LIMPING TO LONDON

AT CHRISTMAS 1829, a Cornish farmer and his wife in Tywardreath near Fowey in Cornwall had their minds less on their Christmas dinner than on an impending addition to the household. Mr and Mrs Lobb were awaiting another baby which was expected daily. The circumstances of the birth are unknown, the first words or noises of the son who was born on December 27th unrecorded, but it requires little imagination to picture a birth probably attended by an amateur village midwife, provided even she could be brought out on a dark December night; the excitement of the event somewhat impaired by the fact that for a decade at least, this was no new breadwinner or labourer for the farm, but another mouth to feed in difficult times.

It may be that the father was not even a farmer but an agricultural labourer, living in a tied cottage, whose labours brought in not profits but a pittance of a wage.

There had been Lobbs in Cornwall since at least the sixteenth century, and another branch of Lobbs had settled in Spitalfields as part of the Huguenot influx of the 1690s stemming from the persecution of French protestants. The Cornish branch of the family had produced a Sheriff and Member of Parliament for a Cornish borough in the seventeenth century, and a number of distinguished theologians and dissenting ministers. Our Mr and Mrs Lobb were, however, of more plebian stock altogether.

Though Cornwall was no further from London then than it is today, it was, as far as communications went, a million

light years away. The main highway between Penzance and
London was not even a road—it was the sea. The last rail
link with the metropolis was not to be completed until thirty
years later in 1859. The natural scenic beauty of the county
should not let us forget that it was, in many ways, a pretty
dangerous place. Hazards abounded: for the unwary there
were tidal marshes, an often turbulent sea, potholes, sudden
fogs, unfenced mine shafts and unsafe or no bridges.

In the eighteenth century, Cornish roads were a by-word
for tangled undergrowth and hidden potholes that could
snap a horse's leg instantly. One lady nearly broke her own
and her horse's neck on a journey to Fowey, and it was in
this region that one of Cornwall's early historians, a Mr
Tonkin, lost his eye to a bramble overhanging the 'road'.

In these circumstances, very few Cornishmen stepped
beyond the limits of their own parish in a lifetime, and
even fewer ever crossed the boundary line of their own
county. Also, this static population was, by and large,
composed of a pretty lawless bunch of individuals. Riddled
with 'pocket' and 'rotten' boroughs, Cornwall in the 1820s
was sending *forty-four* members to an unreformed Westminster.

If baby Lobb was not to follow his father's agricultural
bent, there was little enough choice to offer him. He could
turn to the sea and join the important pilchard industry
centred around Looe, go down the tin-mines which would
have meant travelling over to the Cambourne-Redruth
district, or he could perhaps have joined Fowey's largest
industry of all—smuggling! Frowned on by authorities
from beyond the district and prone to raids by Customs and
Excisemen, smuggling flourished with the smiling cogni-
sance if not the active co-operation of local magistrates.

Fowey's own customs and excisemen were notoriously
corrupt; their posts were held as a kind of goodwill token in
return for assistance and votes at Parliamentary election
time. If a local exciseman showed too much zeal in tracking
down the local smugglers, he would be speedily repri-

manded, or transferred and replaced by a more tolerant agent. In 1824, Fowey had witnessed the richly comic sight of the Lord Mayor himself barring the door to subordinate customs officials, while his servants disposed of his vast store of contraband brandy through the back door of his house.

When young Lobb was six-years-old, he would certainly have been aware of the rumpus in 1835 when five Fowey smugglers were acquitted by a Cornish jury (twelve good men and true?) after a pitched battle with excisemen, on the highly dubious grounds that large sticks and bludgeons did not constitute 'offensive weapons'.

Although by all accounts the young John Lobb was a strong healthy boy, the lure of the sea and the glamour of smuggling may have held no particular appeal; or if they did, his father may have stepped in and decreed, with that finality of judgement against which there can be no filial appeal, that what was good enough for himself would be good enough for his son. John Lobb, at about eleven or twelve, started work on either his father's or his father's employer's farm.

So far as we know, he was happy and in normal circumstances would have eked out a living for the rest of his life from the soil. But, then there came a disaster. According to one account, he fell from the back of an obdurate donkey. According to another, he fell from a hay wagon. Either way, there was no doubt about the result. Not only was the young boy's leg broken in more than one place; crude first aid and bone-setting left the lad with a permanent injury. From now on he could do little more than hobble. His agricultural career was over.

In fact the 'disaster' was the making of his life. Physical disabilities operate differently on different temperaments. To some it becomes a built-in excuse for failure in life and an opportunity for self-pity. To others, it brings a passive acceptance and an ability to make the best of that part of their life that remains unimpaired. But there is another category, those whose courage and whose fighting spirit makes them determined to continue a perfectly normal existence against whatever odds confront them, and to prove to others, or perhaps to themselves, that they can still be pre-eminent in their field. In this category, one must place the Helen Kellers and the Douglas Baders of the world, and also young John Lobb.

Such feelings at this stage of his young life must have been lying dormant, or perhaps were temporarily quashed, for the decision on the boy's new future was taken by his father. It was to apprentice him to a local shoemaker. Any trade that involved mobility or dexterity of foot was clearly out, so in the tiny self-sufficient economy of a Cornish village, it must have been Hobson's choice. For at least the next five years, John Lobb learned the intricacies of bootmaking.

He must have adapted well to the new demands of the gentle craft. There are no records of his master's identity, or of how good a workman or teacher he was, but one piece of John Lobb's own work came to light in 1948. A letter was written to the firm by a Mr John Keast, which ran:

Dear Sir,
    At an exhibition illustrating 'Fowey, Past and Present' held in the Town Hall, Fowey, Cornwall in June last, one of the items on loan was a piece of leather-work with very fine stitches. The owner told me that it was considered a remarkable piece of work in so far as it was hand sewn and consisted of more than 30 stitches to the inch. It has been in his family for a great many years and had been made by a young man named Lobb who was born in Fowey and who had been in his grandfather's employ ...

Tantalisingly, neither the work nor the owner were traced, but circumstantial evidence suggests that the young Lobb was already, in Cornish terms at least, an exceptional craftsman. But there is a great deal of difference between being the best bootmaker in Cornwall, if such he were, and the best bootmaker in the world, which, in the light of his actions during the next few years, is what he was determined to become.

At some time after his apprentice's indentures had been gained, Fowey became too small for John Lobb. He decided to go to London. By this time, not only had his own determination to overcome his old injury grown to almost an obsession, but he had picked up some of the shoemakers' trouble-making temperament at the same time as his skill with awl and bristle.

Fitted out in a pair of his own boots, he journeyed to London, and he went in the only possible way short of paying an inflated and prohibitive fare on a coast-to-coast ship—he walked, or rather limped, the 200-odd miles to the capital.

Knowing what we do of the conditions of the road and the pitfalls which could confront a solitary traveller on a long journey, how one would love to read a diary written on such a journey—today it would have the interest and historical importance of Defoe's or Cobbett's accounts of their travels, if not their literary qualities. Alas, all we know for certain is that he got there.

Now for a small-scale Cornish shoemaker coming into London, where, as we have seen, shoe and bootmakers were two a penny, probably the best he could hope for was to be allowed to help out in some small Regent Street or Oxford Street backroom at the beck and call of a master bootmaker with a number of similar craftsmen under him. This however, was not for John Lobb. He had arrived, not to join such people, but in modern footballing parlance, to take them on.

With the dust and sweat of months of travel on the road to London still clinging to him, John Lobb did not find his way to a small back street or a dingy arcade. Again we have the testimony of our old friend Mayhew as to what those places were like: 'Let us now wander in the Arcade of the Melancholy-Mad Bootmakers, known to Londoners as The Opera Arcade ... It is long, very narrow, and badly lighted, having shops, or rather cells, wholly on one side of it. You rarely see anybody walking in this arcade, and to find a

person in any one of the shops is a still greater novelty....
[We] caught glimpses of shopmen eyeing us furtively from
over the tops of blinds or from behind doors ...' John Lobb,
secure in the knowledge that he was already a master in his
own right, was headed for St James's Street.

Few London streets have the character and history of St
James's, with its gentle hill running up from St James's
Palace to Piccadilly. The street had seen some strange sights
from its days as a preserve of leisured males dividing their
time between the country and the clubs and coffee houses.
Pickering Place is supposed to be the scene of the last London
duel. At 64 had been the Cocoa Tree where hundreds of
thousands of pounds had changed hands on the turn of a
hazard card. One house, successively named Beaufort, Hamilton and Wimborne, had been the home of Prime Minister
Pelham. In 1815, the street had been described thus: '[the
west side] is chiefly composed of stately houses belonging to
the nobility and gentry. The opposite side consists of elegant
shops, which appear to a stranger rather as the lounging-
places than the resorts of trade and the busy pursuits of
merchandise.'

Along its pavements had walked residents like Gillray the
cartoonist, Wren, Gibbon, Pope, Creevey and Byron, and
visitors like the Regency dandies, Beau Brummell and
Horace Churchill, on their way to their bootmaker's. Both
Brummell and Churchill, like the Duke of Wellington, had
their boots made in St James's Street by a London bootmaker and Methodist preacher Hoby 'the Great'. This
unusual man, whose door was clustered with the names of
his many royal patrons, swore that Wellington's victories
had been due to his Hoby boots; he also reprimanded a
customer who complained that his top boots had split with
a 'Good God! You've been walking in them!' and died
leaving a fortune of £120,000.

Outside White's, the coffee and chocolate house and later
club, a club member had died for the want of medical
attention: he had collapsed on the steps, and a doctor had

been prevented from attending to him because the bloods had begun to run a book on his recovery or demise, and outside assistance would have been seen as interfering unfairly with the result!

Hoby the Great was dead and gone like the White's member. The supreme accolade of the top bootmaker in London, and therefore in the world, had moved, but not very far. At 36 St James's Street, was the premises of Thomas's the bootmakers. In later years, they were to be Lobb's greatest rivals, but now they stood alone and supreme. It was straight to Thomas's that young John Lobb headed.

He stumped into the shop, a pair of his own boots in his hands, and before the staff had had time to recover from the sight of this strange travel-worn youth so unlike the regular callers at the august premises, they had been coolly informed that Mr John Lobb of Cornwall had arrived and that Mr John Lobb was not leaving until he had seen old man Thomas himself.

Thomas was, of course, probably as near to a friend of kings and princes as a tradesman was ever likely to be, and for his staff to summon him to see an unknown Cornish youth did nothing for his temper. The result was an unseemly slanging match between the two, with Thomas laughing at the pretensions of John Lobb and ordering him out into the street, but not before John Lobb had shaken a horny Cornish fist in Thomas's face and threatened him with the satisfying exit line of 'I'll build a firm which will knock you sideways!'

Outside in the street, he may have realised how vain a boast he was making—he had no workmen, no customers, no premises, and even with his life's savings secreted about his person, not enough capital to obtain any of them. The one thing he did have was a conviction that if he was not going to be able to work for the best bootmaker in London, he was not going to demean himself by working for any of the lesser lights. He needed money to set himself up in his own premises and he needed it fast. He could not get that by cobbling up some shoddy footwear for the retail trade. In his more rational moments, he must also have realised that he needed experience of the sort of high-class work that a Thomas customer demanded before such a venture as he dreamed of had any chance of success.

By one of those curious coincidences which seem inseparable from the history of Lobb's, this youth, the original John Lobb, had arrived in a London buzzing with rumours of an Eldorado on the other side of the world—gold had been found in Australia and just as in California a year earlier, men as poor as John Lobb had become rich overnight. To become rich overnight would bring his dreams that much nearer fulfilment. His decision was easy: he would go to Australia.

5

THERE'S GOLD IN THEM THAR HEELS

I⊤ WOULD be overstating the case to say that we would not
now recognise the London that John Lobb had visited so
briefly, and was now prepared to leave almost as rapidly
as he had entered, but in many ways it was strikingly
different to the modern city.

Harrod's was a tiny Knightsbridge grocery shop, Trafal-
gar Square had a Nelson's column but no Landseer lions,
Big Ben had not yet been built and the new Houses of
Parliament would not be ready for another twelve months.
The Victorian equivalent of the rush hour was almost as
noisy as our own, with the clatter of hooves and wheels on
cobbles; so it was a kind of betwixt and between city that
John Lobb was leaving, half old and half modern.

What ship he sailed on to the Southern hemisphere
remains unrecorded, but there is a well-known painting
which gives us some idea of the scene. One of the prominent
painters of the Pre-Raphaelite brotherhood, Ford Madox
Brown, joined his fellow artists Rossetti and Holman Hunt,
on a quayside at Gravesend in July 1852. They were bidding
their fond and perhaps lachrymose farewells to Thomas
Woolner, the sculptor and poet, who was forsaking the
charms of the chisel and the pen, to seek his fortune in the
Australian goldfields. By this time, special trains and daily
sailings and outfittings demonstrated the lure of the precious
metal. Ford Madox Brown was sufficiently inspired by the
melancholy scene, as the ship *The Windsor* cast off its moor-
ings with the sculptor and a lady companion huddled

mournfully in the bows, behind them a mixed crowd of emigrants already drinking to their own success at the other end of the voyage, to go home and paint his masterpiece *The Last of England*.

If any painter had immortalised the previous departure of John Lobb, who had had no band of brothers to send him on his way, a more appropriate title would have been *I'll be back*. Square-jawed and determined, he was going to make his fortune and when he returned, the Thomases of the world were going to know all about it. He would make sure of that.

One doubts that John Lobb, as he set out, realised that he was following in the wake of another Englishman, Edward Hammond Hargreaves. Born in Gosport in 1816, Hargreaves grew to an imposing 6 feet 5 inches tall and a massive twenty stones, but he left for Australia in 1832 as a diminutive sixteen-year-old cabin boy. Then there was no thought of Australian gold but, after two years at sea, he settled in Australia and became a squatter, barely able to scratch a living as a farmer. He had, however, something of the Lobb spirit, and a penchant for adventure. When the California diggings opened up, he was one of the first to join the rush. He sailed from Sydney in July 1849 and went to the Californian fields. More fortunate than some, he found gold, but in such a minute quantity, that his total findings did not even cover the face of a threepenny bit.

Disillusioned, like so many of the hopeful prospectors who travelled half way across the globe with a golden dream, he sailed back again to New South Wales. For thousands like him, that was the end of the trail, but not for Hargreaves. On his return he was sufficiently astute to realise that, geologically speaking, parts of New South Wales were remarkably like California. Arriving home in January 1851, he re-equipped himself with a horse or a donkey, and a pick, a trowel and a washpan strapped to his saddle. One month later, at Lewis Ponds Creek, he and his two companions found gold.

Hargreaves' claim to be the first to discover gold in Australia was suspect. There had been other finds in the 1840s, but the then state Governor Gipps was an enlightened man and deliberately suppressed news of the finds. He foresaw the social and economic consequences of the inevitable influx of people drawn from all over the world to his territory by the dream of gold.

Hargreaves' partners were now of a similar bent, not because they had a social conscience, but because they wanted to keep the field to themselves. Hargreaves, however, was more wily. By making the discovery public, not only would the fields be opened up for full exploitation, but he could claim for the find. In all probability he could land himself an easy, well-paid job as administrator, while armies of immigrant prospectors had the back-breaking and soul-destroying toil of actually digging up the gold. With this in mind, he rode all the way to Sydney, brought his discovery to the attention of Gipp's successor Fitzroy and, in case that worthy felt public-spirited enough to quash the news, held a public meeting and wrote a letter to the *Sydney Morning Herald* proclaiming the glad tidings. Five hundred men left the meeting and went straight to the Ophir field. The gold rush had begun.

Hargreaves sat back, collected a handsome reward and was duly appointed Commissioner of Crown Lands, while Fitzroy announced a scheme to license every prospector and to give a fixed price for all gold found.

Soon enough, the news reached London with ships carrying thousands of pounds' worth of gold to prove that this was no idle rumour. Gold mining companies, mostly confidence tricks, mushroomed, more and more ships were fitted, and even the staid *Times* was speaking with a voice of enthusiasm: 'The whole of the newest of the new worlds, that *angulus terrae* so long reserved from man, seems literally golden.'

Whether John Lobb saw a newspaper placard or heard a newsboy shout 'Gold in Australia!' or perhaps limped into a bar where the talk was all of the new Eldorado, we shall never know. All we know is that as soon as he could get a passage, he was bound for Sydney. As he sailed, the flood of diggers to the Ophir doubled daily and, by the time he was on Australian soil, the frenzy had redoubled with the opening of the Macquarie and Turon rivers. It was to the Turon that the master bootmaker, if novice prospector, went.

How many there were just like him can only be guessed, but it is an established fact that the Australian population *tripled* in three years. And even the residents were on the move. From South Australia 10,000, out of a total population of only 70,000, left for Ophir although few ever got there once new findings were made in the State of Victoria. Side by side, in some vast unwashed army, lawyers, magistrates and farmers walked or rode in the company of Tasmanian convicts and unemployed labourers, all hell-bent on easy riches, and falling over each other like gold-dazzled lemmings.

The camp-followers in the wake of this huge hopeful army, the gamblers, the whores, the con-men, the bandits, the illicit whisky-distillers and the tent-robbers, joined the tail of the great march. It was said, 'None are fitted for the diggings who cannot sleep under a tree in the open air, drink waters of all colours, go for a week unwashed and unshaved, and submit to be overrun by vermin.'

This was the grim reality underlying the dream. What bloody and dreadful scenes the young Lobb must have seen. Any prejudices he may have already held about his fellow man would have been amply confirmed. Men's throats were cut as they lay asleep, unlicensed diggers took away legitimate claims at gun point, cholera was rampant, and horrifying tales filtered back to civilisation—of the lucky few finding vast nuggets of gold and lighting their cigars with ten-pound notes, or placing fivers between slices of bread and eating the most expensive sandwiches of their lives; and of the luckless many, scavenging or stealing to keep alive. In one ramshackle store, a human hand was nailed to the wall, an awesome warning to any who tried to repeat its owner's attempt to sneak a handful of bread through the storekeeper's window.

Not long after John Lobb's arrival at the Turon, news broke of the easy pickings to be had at the Ballarat fields near Melbourne. Victoria was the next to get the rag, tag and bobtail army and the Turon fields saw daily parties of liquor-swigging, gun-firing, music-playing desperadoes setting out in carts or on foot for the new Nirvana 400 miles away. He himself had seen enough to treat the latest news with scepticism. He had found no gold, and he was sensible enough to realise that Ballarat would be the scene of similar excesses. He resolved to stay put, not to dig for gold, but to revert to his craft.

This was in its way a discovery to rank with a golden nugget. There were still many thousands of prospectors in the Turon; what better than to supply them with Lobb boots? There were no craftsmen of his ability within hundreds of miles, and who was going to scramble over the Australian outback terrain inadequately shod if they could obtain a pair of stout hard-wearing boots? He had tapped a rich vein of opportunity on which he alone had a monopoly.

The Lobb tent in the Turon may not have had the grandeur of a mahogany-fronted premises in St James's Street, but it did a roaring trade. In came the prospectors with clogs or rags around their feet, and out they went again in a decent pair of boots, only too ready to exchange some of their dust or their nuggets for the privilege.

His ambitions grew in parallel with his pile of gold. He then had another brilliant idea. He designed and made a prospector's boot. This was to all outward appearances just like his other boots, but hidden skilfully in the construction was a hollow heel which slid away from the sole to provide a secret and safe-like compartment to conceal nuggets and dust. Better than a money belt or a pouch, prospectors could now literally walk around on their fortune. Orders and sales doubled.

At about this time, he heard news from one of the other fields that his own brother, William, who he knew was in Australia but had no idea of his whereabouts, was lying gravely ill a few hundred miles away. His fraternal concern took an eminently practical turn. From his earnings he took enough money to buy a horse and a bottle of port, and rode post-haste for his brother's side. The Australian horse was more co-operative than the Cornish donkey of his childhood, and got him there safely and in time to force the bottle of port down his brother's throat. The port, the nearest thing to medicine available in such parts, did the trick and the brother recovered.

His angel of mercy stint completed, back went John Lobb to the Turon and, for probably a year, he continued to shoe the Turon hopefuls with the Lobb prospector's boot; so successfully that the time came when he could take saddle-bags full of gold and ride back to Sydney a relatively rich man without ever finding one morsel of gold on his own account. Hargreaves, had he known of Lobb's existence, must have heartily approved.

In Sydney, he cashed in all his gold at the fixed government price of £3 4s an ounce and bought a shop in George Street. The first part of his ambitions, to have his own firm in his own right, had been fulfilled.

George Street, Sydney, was one of the main shopping centres of the day; small tailors, grocers, watchmakers, stationers, booksellers, carpet warehouses, whip-makers and ironmongers stood side by side competing with each other and with street traders like the legendary Flying Pieman (who sounds as fictional as the Topless Aborigine or the Pink Kangaroo Australians reserve for gullible tourists). Few of them would have been craftsmen in their own right and they battled in dockside auctions for goods imported from abroad as they were unloaded from the ships.

When the prospectors or squatters hit town for their

annual shopping spree, George Street must have been a lively place. Knowing that the visitors might spend up to £2,000 in an afternoon, the wine shops allowed free sampling of their wines, and the other traders got the benefit of the alcohol-induced largesse. Since 1851, more than one thousand million pounds' worth of gold has come out of Australia, and naturally there were many who wanted to tap such riches at source. The new premises with the imposing title, John Lobb, Bootmaker, was in a good place.

The ex-prospector now turned his full attention to his bootmaking craft. What to many people would have been an arrival, to him was merely a stopping place *en route* to his real goal—to get back to London and to replace Thomas as the world's leading bootmaker. Although he employed others, he continued to work himself on boots for customers, patiently improving his already outstanding skill.

Almost incidentally, he became one of Sydney's leading tradesmen. He grew a dark, handsome beard and dressed with a measure of elegance befitting his new social position. He also attracted the attention of the Sydney Harbour-master's daughter, a Miss Richards, and after going through the social obligations of courtship he married her in 1857. They had children, first a son, John, in 1858, then two girls, Caroline Victoria in 1859 and Mary Aline in 1861. But despite his growing family, he had no intensions of settling down.

One of the very few actual documents still extant which relate to John Lobb dates from this period in Australia. Partly damaged by age, it is the indenture relating to the apprenticeship to John Lobb of his wife's younger brother Frederick Richards in 1863, which stated:

This indenture witnesseth.
Sydney	That I, Frederick Moses Richards, Son of
New South Wales	Thomas Richards, of his own free will and
	accord and with the consent of his parents,
doth put himself an indoor apprentice to John Lobb Bootmaker

of Sydney in the Colony of New South Wales to learn his art
and with him (after the manner of an apprentice) to serve from the
twenty fourth-day of April One thousand Eight hundred and sixty
three untill [sic] the full end of a term of five years and nine
months from thence next following to be fully completed and
ended, during wich [sic] term the said apprentice his said master
faithfully shall serve, his secrets keep his lawfull [sic] commands
everywhere gladly do. He shall do no damage to his said master,
not see it done by others but that he shall forthwith give warning
to his said Master of the same, he shall not waste the goods of his
said master not lend or give them unlawfully to any. He shall
neither buy or sell without his said master's leave. Taverns, Inns,
Playhouses he shall not haunt. At Cards, dice tables, or any other
unlawful games he shall not play. Matrimony he shall not contract,
nor from the service of his said Master day or night absent himself, but in all things as a faithful apprentice, he shall behave
himself towards his said Master and all his family during the
said Term.

The said John Lobb doth hereby covenant with the said Thomas
Richards that the said John Lobb his said Apprentice in the Art
of Boot Closing and all things appertaining thereto wich [sic]
he noeth [sic] by that best means that he can, shall teach and
instruct or cause to [be] taught and instructed, Finding unto the
said apprenticeship Board Lodging and Clothing during the said
Term.

And for the true performance of all and every [one of the]
said covenants and agreements either of the said parties bindeth
himself unto the other by the Presents.

In Witness whereof the parties above named to these Indentures
have put their hands and seals at Sydney in the Colony of New
South Wales the Twenty fourth day of April in the year of our
Lord One Thousand Eight hundred and Sixty three.

Signed Sealed and delivered
by the above named Frederick
Moses Richards Thomas   F. M. Richards
Richards and   &
John Lobb   Thos Richards
in the presence of   &
Daniel Young   John Lobb

This document gives a clear indication of the lot of an
apprentice, beholden to his master for everything but the

right to draw breath, and perhaps that was covered by unwritten house rules. The point is that John Lobb, in his first business venture, was not a Robert Owen concerned primarily with his workers' welfare, but neither was he an exploiter or sweat-shop owner. He was just a man of his time, no better, no worse, than thousands of others. But what a marvellous insight it gives us to contemporary opinions as to what rights and duties were expected from master and man. The most casual comparison with a modern contract of employment will show how industrial relations have changed since the days of the first Lobb.

6

FAME . . . BY APPOINTMENT

IN so many ways, progress during the nineteenth century was a gloomy business for the majority of the working population. Success rested upon competition—competition not alleviated by state interference, but allowed frequently to reduce the profits of the employer and the wages of his workmen to alarmingly low levels.

Under the influence of contemporary opinion confirmed by evangelical doctrines, all this seemed as inevitable as the workings of nature itself. Only by industry and abstinence could the master increase his sales, and only by work and thrift could the employee hope to stay above the bread-line. Virtue alone brought its just economic reward.

However, when harsh facts of economic life brought depression or a change in the terms of trade, the virtuous went under with the idle and the indolent; most of those who shared the opinion of Victorian society were on a gently but steadily rising tide of economic prosperity which confirmed all their beliefs and prejudices. Not for nothing was the sermon the mass-media equivalent of its day.

This is important because it allows us to see John Lobb as a man of his time. He was no social reformer, neither was he a grinder of the faces of the poor. Neither was he a hypocrite who preached standards for others he was disinclined to follow himself. Like others of his kind, he took life as he found it, and by dint of his supreme belief in his own skill as a craftsman and a competitive temperament forged in a hard school, he carved out the best niche for himself that he could.

His workmen had to produce shoes and boots of the highest class or they would not be Lobb workmen for long. He was only putting on them the sort of demands he always put upon himself, and when they responded to the challenge he was prepared to reward them fairly. He well knew he could make boots far and above Australian standards, but he could only progress to his large aims by making them to world standards. By 1862, he had the perfect opportunity to step on to a larger stage.

The Great Exhibition of 1851, staged in London under 18¼ acres of glass, had drawn some six million people. In 1862, London repeated the experiment and a sixteen-and-a-half acre site, lying approximately between Prince Albert's Road, Exhibition Road and Cromwell Road, was devoted to the new exhibition. From all over the world, applications to exhibit in the many classes, which ranged from naval architecture and sanitary appliances to fine art and agriculture, poured in—9,862 of them, to be exact. Each of the colonies were awarded a section of the space, and at the end of the British nave on the corner of the Eastern dome was an area devoted to the products of New South Wales. Alongside was a forty-foot high gold pyramid proclaiming Victoria's prominence as the most highly developed of the Australian territories. But New South Wales, its 336,572 population already providing an external commerce of over £11 million—a large amount for an area not founded until 1788—was a clear second. New South Wales showed nuggets, quartz, gold, coins from the Sydney mint and a host of other products, including footwear.

Class 27, Section D was devoted to boots and shoes. It was judged by an international jury composed of two London bootmakers, one London shoemaker, an Austrian leather manufacturer, and the Directors of the Chambers of Commerce of Stuttgart and of France. Their report shows the increased attention the industry was now receiving:

In the Exhibition of 1851, it [*i.e.* footwear] formed part of a class with a large variety of other descriptions of goods ... and consequently the same amount of interest was not drawn to it as on the present occasion, when it has been found necessary to allot a special section and Jury to this trade alone; the large number of contributions from all parts of the world demanding such an arrangement. The Juries in their labours have had to decide upon the merits of no less than 328 manufacturers ... from thirty seven countries.

Clearly not only John Lobb had his eyes on becoming the world's top craftsman. The greatest competition was from England and from technological developments, as the Jury makes clear:

... The great perfection now attained by the manufacturers of 'machine-closed uppers' is worthy of note, as being since the last Exhibition an entirely new branch of the trade, and one which, for the export and wholesale market, appears capable of large results. As a whole, the exhibition of the English trade must be taken as a vast improvement upon that of the year 1851.

As one would expect from this, England took a lion's share of 25 medals, with six going to Austria and four to India, but one gold medallist was the sole Australian winner: '364 LOBB, J. GOOD WORK AND FIRST-CLASS MATERIALS'

John Lobb had proved that his work was up to world standards which were themselves on the up and up. As the jury's report states, '... the display now brought under their [the jury's] notice is one that does great credit to the Exhibitors, not only as regards the excellence of the goods but also as indicating the progress made ... since the Exhibition of 1851.

Interestingly enough, one of the jurors, Box, was destined to be taken over in later years by the Australian-Cornish upstart.

His ambition fed by the award, John Lobb now made a sustained and infinitely more subtle attack on London than his abortive and impudent assault of a decade before. This time, it was a cunning and persistent campaign that eventually bore fruit.

First he took infinite pains to make a superb pair of riding boots, from the very best-quality hide and hand-sewn with fine stitching of the kind that has become legendary in the trade. Placing them in an impressive leather box he sent them to London, to the Prince of Wales. Together with the boots went a request to be appointed as bootmaker to the Prince.

One can only speculate how on earth a man in Australia was able to obtain the measurements of the Royal feet, but, in the words of John Lobb's grandson, he was 'wily enough for anything'. This piece of early industrial espionage paid off. The Prince was sufficiently impressed to afford John Lobb, the coveted award of a Royal Warrant as his bootmaker. The application meeting with royal approval, or perhaps amusement at the Lobb effrontery, it passed through the official channels, and a Warrant was issued by Lord Chamberlain Knollys on October 12th 1863. The document now hangs framed in the Lobb premises in St James's Street together with the photograph of its grantor.

The coveted Royal Warrants carry an enormous amount of prestige, putting a final seal on the arrival of the tradesman in fashionable circles. Since one Thomas Herbert had been granted permission to style himself 'Their Majesties' Clockmakers in Ordinary' in 1692, many a warrant had been issued, not only to brush-, whisky- and biscuit-manufacturers and the like, but also to bagpipe-makers, reed-thatchers and chimney-sweeps.

Victorian times brought many abuses of the privilege, reaching some sort of nadir with a firm including in an advertisement a copy of the Queen's order for a case of Raggett's Nourishing Stout. Queen Victoria issued her own Royal Warrants, but some sources say that she was never over-fond of allowing her Consort or her son to do the same. Was the issue to John Lobb a piece of the Prince of Wales' defiance against his mother? Did he think that a tradesman

in Australia would escape her notice? Or did he think the
Lobb boots so superior that he felt he could steal a march
over his London-shod contemporaries?

The future Edward VII, at the time the warrant was
issued, was beginning to throw off the strait-jacket of his
education and upbringing preparatory to becoming the
leader of a fashionable and pacy set. Two years before there
had been the scandal of his visit to the Curragh when an
actress had been smuggled into his quarters. Six months
before, he had married Princess Alexandra of Schleswig-
Holstein-Sonderburg-Blucksburg and, as Disraeli put it, it
was a Royal honeymoon extended over months. If the Lobb
riding boots were not an unsolicited wedding present, at
least they arrived at a time which Sir Philip Magnus, the
Prince's biographer (and a Lobb customer himself) describes
so beautifully as, '... such a season as London had never
previously known ... As ball succeeded ball amid a whirl of
fêtes and receptions, processions and ceremonies, the Prince
of Wales, in the flower of his lusty youth and with the most
beautiful Princess in Europe at his side, inaugurated, with
startling suddenness and inimitable gusto, a social sover-
eignty which endured until he died.'

Queen Victoria was none too pleased at her son's emergence as a leader of society, but the Prince's healthy dislike
of arrogance and snobbery served to condition both Society
and the monarchy to the changing times. In Magnus's
words, he 'secured the foundations of the monarchy deep
in public opinion'.

The custom of the Prince and his set was the one thing
which could secure John Lobb's final arrival on the London
scene, and armed with the prestigious document, and a less
than modestly-sized coat of arms to place above his shop-
front, Lobb sold his business in Australia to another bootmaker who continued as Lobb and Hampley (they are no
longer in business) and, with his young apprentice Frederick
Richards, sailed for London at some time during 1866.

His wife and his three young children were left behind

in Sydney; they were to be summoned to follow when he had successfully secured premises in the West End. It is not thought to have been the happiest of marriages, so the enforced temporary separation may well have freed Lobb's mind to concentrate on this new furthering of his ultimate ambition.

His first appearance in the London Post Office Directory is in the 1867 Edition, which would have been prepared during 1866, so we can reasonably believe that John Lobb, Bootmaker was first in London in 1866. He took over premises at 296 Regent Street which had been previously occupied by Leroy and Son, watch and clock makers, so it must have taken him a few months to refit the workshops and shop interior to his own exacting standards. At last he was in London and in business, and as the coat of arms flamboyantly displayed over the front window made clear, catering for the highest possible class of customers.

This would not have been true of many of his neighbours clamouring for attention in the Regent Street of the 1860s. There were a dozen other bootmakers, hosts of tailors and milliners, but also a glorious selection of weird and wonderful tradesmen who have long since disappeared into oblivion. Regent Street then boasted of a horse feed depot, a revalenta arabica food importer (who supplied a food made from lentils and barley flour), a chiropodist, an artist, an Italian sculpture importer, a magical repository, a French colza oil depot, a wax bleacher and a concertina maker.

More seriously to John Lobb, the directory also shows that there were 3,171 bootmakers in London *other* than wholesale suppliers. That makes for a lot of competition when you intend to be the best.

Tragically, all the sales ledgers and order books of this period were destroyed by an over-zealous manager in later years, so we do not know what nineteenth-century giants found their way to 296 Regent Street. But we do know that John Lobb made at least one friend among his fellow tradesmen, if not among more aristocratic circles. This was the owner and proprietor of a silk mercer and linen drapers which extended from 103 to 108 Oxford Street. His friend, Peter Robinson, for such was he, had a money-spinning subsidiary at 256 to 262 Regent Street—a mourning warehouse upon which much of his growing business depended.

If this sounds an odd claim, let us remember the Victorian attitude to bereavement. Whereas in biblical times Job had rent his mantle, Victorian widows lost their bread-winners with an altogether more refined style of domestic display. Grief went for nothing if it was not fashionable. In this new-style luxury of woe, garments were rent to order, sackcloth was of the finest quality and mantles tended to be made of splendid quality at eighteen shillings a yard. And for supplying the necessary equipment for the ceremony, the Peter Robinsons of the world reaped handsome profits.

Robinson was a generous man, and he on more than one occasion helped John Lobb's finances, overstrained by the expense of a move half-way across the world, with the occasional helpful loan to pay a quarterly bill, or to settle an outstanding leather merchant's account. At a time when many of his three thousand competitors closed for the want of a similar temporary hand-out, John Lobb was eternally grateful to his new friend. Travellers in today's West End will see that the loans did Peter Robinson no harm either.

Duly established in Regent Street, the living quarters of which had been handsomely furnished in contemporary style, John Lobb then sent for his wife and children. Unaccompanied, except for the children who were unhelpfully stricken with measles during the three-month voyage, she eventually joined her husband at 296 Regent Street. The reunion was at least temporarily successful for they had two more sons, William Hunter born in June 1870 and Frederick in September 1871, and a daughter, Flora, who did not survive infancy. Frederick also met an untimely end for he died in 1890 at the age of nineteen of appendicitis, or as it was then described 'stoppage of the bowels'.

It was not a permanent reconciliation however. His wife

separated from him and she spent her last days living in
Paris where she died and was buried, thousands of miles
away from her Sydney home. She could not have been a
happy woman. Probably she was never sufficiently part of
his real obsession—his craft and his ambition—and in
these pre-Women's Lib days, she came low down on the
list of his priorities.

In this London where there were more Irishmen than in
Dublin, more Jews than in Palestine, more Roman Catholics
than in Rome, and more Scotsmen than in Aberdeen, John
Lobb both worked and played exceedingly hard. In addition
to the normal course of making customers' boots, and it
must be remembered that a workman of this period had to
make at least six pairs of boots in a week to feed a family,
which took even a fast worker about seventy-two hours; John
Lobb also continued to give attention to the making of
boots purely for exhibition.

As a tradesman and an uneducated man, he would have
neither felt at ease in the social circles of his customers, nor,
for that matter, been able to move in such circles had he
wanted to. He made money the hard way and then spent
it with the relish of a man with a clear conscience. He lived
well and within his own society gained a reputation as a
bit of a gay dog. He preferred the country to the town, but
one doubts that that precluded the odd night out at the
music hall where the drink flowed as freely as the melodies.

He used his money to support his large family at 296
Regent Street, an establishment which included his one
time apprentice and later workman, Frederick Richards, and
to travel. He returned to his Cornish village often, where
the younger residents speculated that his limp might be
due to a wooden leg, and was content to bask in the glory
of being the local boy who had made good by leaving the
village. He organised Cornish wrestling matches, put up
prizes, and even became something of a local philanthropist,
slipping the odd sovereign discreetly into the pocket or the
purse of one or other of the older residents.

He took a holiday in America, the only surviving memento of the trip being a photograph of himself and some companions against the imposing background of Niagara Falls, the expressions on their faces suggesting that much else besides Niagara had flowed during the course of the afternoon. He is not grinning in the picture but he could surely be forgiven for an inward smile in the knowledge that his skill and his adventuring spirit had brought him the wealth and even a measure of fame that, to a small boy with a badly broken leg, must have looked as elusive as a moonbeam.

7

AWARDS AND 'PUSSENTIDGES'

THE LAST half of the nineteenth century and the early part of the twentieth was a period in which the boot and shoe industry in general came to terms with the Industrial Revolution which had changed not only the face of British industry but the entire British way of life. It came to the factory system late compared with hundreds of other similar handcrafts, but not all of the painful mistakes made while these earlier trades changed were avoided. The bootmaking trade had its Luddites, its labour and union troubles and disputes, and saw many bankruptcies and injustices as it reformed itself into a modern industry.

The wholesale trade of 1850, small as it was, had factories but did not have power. A machine, invented by D. M. Randolph and improved by the elder Brunel, had riveted soles to uppers at relatively high speeds under the increased demands for cheap boots caused by the French Wars of the early years of the century. However, with the end of the Wars came the end of the demand, and in peacetime the machine fell from use and then from memory.

The pattern of making in factories of the mid-century was to cut out upper leathers carefully and sole leathers roughly, and send them out to home-based makers or 'binders' as they were called. These workmen, often masters in their own right, sometimes took on apprentices and operated to all intents and purposes in the same way as a bespoke bootmaker like John Lobb.

By 1856, the American Singer Company was selling a

sewing machine to British factories but this was powered by a clumsy foot treadle. At about the same time that a British factory owner, William Clark, was developing his own machine for building up and attaching heels, other American firms were pushing cutting and stamping out machines, but these too depended for their motor power upon an operative's foot.

Taking up Adam Smith's famous example of the division of labour so far as pins are concerned, the Americans continued to find methods of treating boots like pins. British manufacturers followed in their footsteps, but even in the 1890s this was still not a fully powered industry. In fact, Sir John Clapham, the economic historian, records that in 1871 there was only 400 horsepower of steam in 145 factories.

Despite continuing influxes of American machines from the 1880s onwards, a town like Leeds still had half the work of making done at home, and London remained an area where there were so many out-workers that satisfactory statistics of earnings were impossible to compile with any degree of certitude. The trend however was for the factory-hand to be taking the work away from the masters and workmen at home. This latter group, weakened by their small numbers, were unable to form a strong trade union to protect their interests. Despite this, the period from 1895 to 1905, which saw the industry at last equipped with powered machinery for high quality work in nearly all its processes, began with a bitter and prolonged national lock-out.

One can see why all too easily. The technical changes had reduced the demand for skill, eased the entry to the trade of the less skilled, and brought a flood of pauper immigrants exploited by ruthless employers because they were accustomed to working for much lower wages than the indigent workman.

There was a parallel effect upon the ranks of the masters. In the late 1880s and early 1890s, a new class of manu-

Lobb's first London premises – 296 Regent Street – with a less than modest coat of arms. The figure in the centre is William Hunter Lobb as a boy apprentice

55 St James's Street, home of the firm until the Second World War. The white lines on the window panes are strips of sticking plaster to reduce damage from bomb blast. In the event, they failed dismally

LONDON AND PROVINCIAL
Union of Band=Sewn Boot and Shoe makers.

STATEMENT of WAGES for MEN'S WORK paid by

JOHN LOBB, 296, Regent Street.
MAY, 1907.

Patent butchers calf feet 15/-

LONG BOOT MAKING.

	s.	d.
Jockey Boots or Wellingtons	13	6
Butcher Boots	13	6
Regulations, Napoleons, or Jacks, ¼ heel ..	14	6
Field Boots, caps 6d. extra	12	6
Hessians, Holderness, or Thigh Boots	14	6

SPECIAL EXTRAS ON LONG WORK.

	s.	d.
Patent, Enamel, Russet or Cloth Legs, with Patent Fronts	2	0
Ditto ditto, Calf Fronts	1	0
Patent, Enamel, Russet, Kid, or Paniscorium Fronts ..	1	0
Double or Stiff Legs	0	6
Spur Rest if put on by Maker	1	0

SHORT BOOT MAKING.

	s.	d.
Button, Lace, or Springside Boots or Shoes	11	0
Military Springs	11	6
Ditto, Patent	12	6
Tie or Buckle Shoe, with Patent Vamp over Instep ..	12	0
Slipper Shoes	10	6
Pumps	9	6
Tennis Shoes, Lasting and Welting, straps 6d. extra..	5	0

SPECIAL EXTRAS ON SHORT WORK.

	s.	d.
Patent, Enamel, Russet, Kid or Paniscorium Fronts	0	6
Patent, Enamel, Russet, Silk or Stockingette Legs ..	0	6
Prunella, Cloth, Canvas, or Chamois Legs ..	0	6
Brown Boots, one material all through..	1	0
Silk or Prunella all through	0	6
Caps, Crup or Circular extra	0	6
Cricket Straps	0	6
Ditto Spikes	0	6
Ditto, ditto, if rivetted by Maker	1	0
Ditto, ditto, Improved Plate	1	6

GENERAL EXTRAS ON LONG OR SHORT WORK.

	s.	d.
Box Toes	1	0
Channel Waist	0	6
Springs in Waist	0	6
Insole Turned up in Waist	0	6
Welt or Rand Corks..	2	6
Seat Corks, 1 inch or under, each	1	6
Ditto, every ¼ inch above 1 inch, each	0	3
Inside Corks as Socks	1	0
Scotch Corks, or Double Sole Corks	1	6
Cork between Soles as Filling	0	6

	s.	d.
Cork all through, fitted by Maker, up to 1 inch ..	2	6
Lined with Fur	1	0
Ditto Cloth, Silk, or Flannel	0	6
Fur Socks	0	6
Waterproofing with Wax or Rubber Solution	0	6
Indiarubber between Soles or Vamps if Stitched in ..	0	6
Aerolite Soles (if Stitched round 1s. extra) ..	1	6
Scafes Soles or Sheet Rubber	1	6
Single Soles, ⅞ in substance	0	6
Double Soles	1	0
Ditto through Waist	1	0
Square Clumps	1	6
Bevel Clumps	2	0
Nails in Toes or Joints	0	6
Hob Nails	0	6
Ditto in Clusters	0	9
Ditto Screwed in or Clinched	1	0
McAfee's Patent Socket and Screws	1	6
Toe or Heel Tips or Plates, putting on.. ..	0	6
Tacks or Fitters in Heels	1	0
Spur Boxes (Latchford's, 1s. 6d.)	1	6
Heels, every ½ of an inch above 1½ inch in height ..	0	3
Wide Welts		
Half-Wide Welts		
Seats Stitched in Short Work	0	6

WORK TO BE TRIED ON BY CUSTOMER.

	s.	d.
One Boot sent into Shop	0	9
Ditto, if Re-lasted to Joint afterwards	1	3
A Pair, if sent into Shop	1	6
Ditto, Re-lasting to Joint afterwards	2	6

Lasting and Sewing, half-wages including extras.
If Finished by another Maker, 1s. extra to half-wages.

ALTERATIONS AND REPAIRING.

Re-lasting or Re-seating half-wages of Making.

	s.	d.
Soleing, Heeling, and Welting	5	9
Soleing and Heeling (Under Heel 6d. extra)	4	0
Soleing (if Stitched on Old Welts 6d. extra)	2	9
Heeling (Lifts per pair 2d. extra)	1	4
Toe Piecing	1	6
Spur Boxes Inserted in Old Heels	3	7
Piecing or Putting Gores in Insoles	0	6
New Toe Caps	0	6
Ditto if not Welted in	0	9
Ditto, Patent	1	2
Patch Stuck on	0	4
Ditto, if Sewed down	0	6

Other Extras same as New Work.
Cork, Tips, Plates, Hob Nails, etc., to be found or paid for by Employer.

Anything not mentioned in this Statement to be Paid for according to time necessary to do the work, or custom of the shop.

The scale of rates paid to outworkers in 1907. A good worker could make perhaps three pairs of boots a week facturer was entering the trade. Some were resolute self-made individualists of the John Lobb stamp. Many of the new machine owners were men like him in that they had learned their craft in the old school. But, unlike him, they switched their attentions to the new machines. They retained their respect for workmanship and worker alike, and prospered.

But there were others. Some who had risen from the ranks of the ordinary workman to become employers showed their contempt for those less fortunate than themselves. This sort of man had a tendency 'to flaunt himself and his position offensively before those whom circumstances had placed under him'. And there were others of the 'get-rich-quick' variety who had little interest in the craft, but saw a chance to profit from something new, and had the minimum of capital available to buy a couple of the new machines. In the 1870s, the *Boot and Shoe Reporter* was carrying advertisements for a Jackson sewing-machine at £50 which the advertisers claimed 'a youth can learn in hours'.

Many did not get rich quick, but got poorer even quicker. In the *Boot and Shoe Reporter* a monthly page of recorded bankruptcies running at fifty a month tells its own sad tale The paper carried a mock toast to shoemakers ('May they wax strong and their soles join in an upper sphere'), but for those affected by the failure of firm after firm, the toast would have been a sick joke.

In the pages of the trade paper insecurity, ruin and fear of the collapse of banks was well nigh universal. Bad debts were often part of the problem. As the *Reporter* sarcastically put it, 'There are several men at the present time whose memories only reach to their knees, and therefore they never pay for their boots.'

When a shop failed, its employees and its outworkers had their livelihoods taken away. Many a Lobb outworker must have offered up thankful prayers that he was working for a master who continued to prosper, and continued to prosper moreover by turning his back on the machine, and for one who was becoming a legend for the highest possible class of hand-made article.

There is plenty of outside evidence that this reading of John Lobb's career is accurate. The first award at the 1862 Exhibition had merely whetted his appetite for more honours. There was such an atmosphere of enthusiasm for mastery of the craft that not only did country compete with country and employer with employer, but the men ran private prize competitions in the public houses between themselves with all the attendant excitement and shouting of odds one would expect from pigeon-fancying or whippet-racing.

I am indebted to Jim Saunders, now Lobb's longest serving workman, for his recalling for me the environment in which his grandfather operated.

The great meeting house and bootmakers' unofficial club was a public house in Berwick Street. There the men met on a Monday for a drink and a discussion of the state of the market. In this masonry of the boot, it was essential to hold a union card or the word that you were a scab would filter around and no work would be forthcoming from any direction. Closers and makers recommended each other at the various West End shops and a call at the pub would indicate what work was available at present.

This tiny trade union, the West End Makers and Closers, not only protected the interests of their members: they had a large and weighty say in the upholding of the standards of their craft. A shoddy piece of work turned in by a workman frequently resulted in a visit to the home of the offender, not from a representative from the master, but from the man from the union who would have some very apposite questions to ask. The union circulated a list of members within their ranks and copies would be sent to the employers too. If a man was in arrears or had been guilty of some other misdemeanour, the facts would appear alongside his name.

Employers could call in a man from the union and complain to him when errors had been made in work. Equally, the union member could call upon the serivces of the union to represent him when he felt he had been unjustly treated by an employer. It was seen by man, employer and union, that they all had a common interest in upholding the craft and in sharing, on a just basis, the rewards for the respective skills and enterprises of the men involved. This, at a time when Capital and Labour were entrenching themselves into rigid postures for bloody and costly struggles, is a shining example of what can be done by the retention of good will to keep up the personal relationship between master and man that had existed since the time of the medieval guilds.

I must not, however, paint too rosy a picture of Arcadian craftsmen dedicated twenty-four hours a day to the greater glory of thread and leather. The other kind of shoemakers' tradition had not died; it was alive and well and residing temporarily in Berwick Street.

The more sober and dedicated maker, if he had work in hand, would be well advised to stay clear of Berwick Street while his luck lasted. Once inside the pub, beer would flow, round after round would be bought, stories would be swapped and the maker would be wending his painful and unsteady way home, too drunk to remember who wanted what on the morrow, and a guarantee of too thick a head to tackle his breakfast let alone fine stitching by candle-light.

And men being men, a common practice would be to go along to a shop which catered for the high-class trade with a pair of boots made not by the applicant for work himself, but by a better craftsman altogether. Some fine pairs, until they were too familiar not to be recognised, did service all over the West End as examples of the work of many a different pair of hands. Of course, unless the applicant could more or less match their quality in the first pair he did make himself for the shop, the workflow stopped there. As firm as any theatrical agent's 'Don't call us, we'll call you', the bespoke bootmaker's dismissal line was 'Thank you, we'll send you a card if there is anything', and away went the worker knowing full well that there never would be.

Even the best of the craftsmen, in which group we can include the present Saunders, his father, and his grandfather, all of them called Jim and known in their times for the purpose of easier identification as Jim, Old Jim and Bloody Old Jim, would be prone to such esoteric practices as 'killing a pair' and 'going on the fuddle'. These customs were, and possibly still are, as quaint as their titles.

'Killing a pair' was to be given an order for a pair of boots or shoes from the shop and to be paid in advance. So far as earning any more money was concerned, this pair of unmade boots was 'dead'. How much easier therefore, to concentrate on making a new pair which would be paid for on delivery, and to let the first order R.I.P. without the formality of a decent burial, hoping that the shop would, in the fullness of time, forget about the departed.

'Going on the fuddle' was a grand extension of another ritual. Unless times were particularly hard, no one worked on Monday—Black or Cobblers' Monday as it was sometimes known. That was a day of escape from the tedium of every other day of the week into the joys of the world of the spirit, or more accurately, the spirits (alcoholic that is). The 'fuddle' meant to be be-fuddled. Some men avoided the Monday and stuck to their last: men like Jim Saunders *père* and Jim Saunders *grand-père*. While their fellows drank away their problems of a Monday, the Saunders carried on working. But ...

Grandfather Saunders had a drawer in his workbench. When he returned with payments for shoes and boots, he opened the drawer and threw the sovereigns inside. As weeks went by, he would open the drawer, mutter 'coming on' to himself, until the gold coins formed an impressive pile. Then, the mutter would turn to a firm 'That's it, I'm off on the fuddle'. Out came the coins, down went the tools, and Bloody Old Jim had finished work for as long as the money lasted. For three weeks or more he would be on a fuddle, the length and intake of which would have made the *Guinness Book of Records*, had that publication then existed. The most urgent orders or the most pressing business had to wait. B.O.J. was on the fuddle and that was it. He and many others did this while their assistants and apprentices had to carry on as best they could.

This sort of quaint custom was understood by John Lobb, and he took them in his stride as part of the hazards of his chosen profession. For the sake of a little understanding and tolerance on his part, he was repaid handsomely by getting work from these men that became world famous. Just as his successors have had to do right up to the present day, he turned a blind eye to the odd 'dead' pair of boots and the occasional temporary disappearance of some of his best craftsmen, and got from them some of the finest hand-made exhibition boots the world has ever seen.

To add to his 1862 medal, he won another at Paris in 1867. At Vienna in 1873 he took a *Fortschritte-medaille* by way of a rehearsal for the International American Centennial Exhibition at Philadelphia. The American judges awarded him another medal and a certificate, commenting: 'A very superior exhibit of werkmanship [*sic*], style and proportions—consisting of gentlemen's dress, walking, shooting, fishing, hunting, riding boots, with patent calf gaiter, Calf —— grain high and strap shoes. Extra stiching [*sic*]; and workmanship very elaborate.

'Laidies [*sic*] gaiter ——, very fine ——. The workmanship can not be surpassed in any country ...' (Blanks indicate illegibility in the original document).

By 1878, it was Paris again and a *medaille d'argent*, and whether winning only the silver stung him into further action or not, he sent another display to the Paris Exhibition of 1889. This won him another gold medal and a report from the English Artisans' Mansion House Committee which saw the work before it went off to represent Britain in France. This report, headed 'Quality of work, difference in make, and materials employed', speaks in glowing terms:

Mr JOHN LOBB of London, exhibits a splendid case of high class hand-made work, comprising nearly every variety of ladies' and gentlemen's hunting, riding, shooting, walking and dress boots and shoes, which for the excellence of material used and superior work-manship, are unequalled in the whole Exhibition; and what materially enhances the value of the exhibit in a practical sense is, that each pair of boots were made on lasts in common use by the firm for customers in their usual course of business.* The style of uppers and shape of the bottoms show excellent judgement and taste, and represent the present fashion in boots and shoes as worn by the nobility and wealthy classes of society, who have not, as this case of work shows, given way as a general rule to that senseless crippling fashion of extremely narrow-pointed shoes. The cutting, closing and making are, in every feature that constitutes best work, exceptionally good, highly creditable to the workmen and employer whose well-deserved high-reputation and world-wide fame is so worthily maintained. The very high skills and taste required to produce such work not only gives a crushing reply to the people who preach about the want of the qualities in our workmen, but also shows that with all the improvements in modern appliances for producing boots by machinery, what a wide distinction still exists between work produced by hand and that produced by machinery.

Rarely can even John Lobb's abilities have been so highly praised, or his business judgement have been so thoroughly vindicated.

For good measure, he sent more work to the Chicago Exhibition of 1893 to win the two highest awards given. It was noted by two jurors that the awards were, firstly 'For fine custom boots and shoes for ladies and gentlemen. The riding boots are of superior quality. Commended for good materials, excellent workmanship and correct proportions;' and secondly, 'For fine workmanship, use of best materials, superior finish, advanced styles, and light weight of walk-ing shoes.'

---

* It was common for exhibition boots to be made on small lasts purely as exercises in stitching, etc.

Sadly, Chicago was the last triumph of the founder's lifetime for he died two years later, but he may rest content in that his firm picked up medals in two Paris Exhibitions in 1900 and 1937 as if he were still around. What is more, he had become the best bootmaker in the world in his own times, and seen the justice of his own obstinate belief in his abilities proved beyond a shadow of doubt. I wonder if the Prince of Wales ever knew to what extent he had helped John Lobb along the way. He must have had some idea, for he was certainly sufficiently aware of goings on in tradesmen's circles to speak out on one occasion against a common malpractice of gentlemen's valets.

Apparently, John Lobb and other West End bootmakers and tailors and the like were occasionally 'taken for a ride' by valets who called to settle their masters' accounts. These enterprising individuals operated a percentage system. A laboured Victorian report declared that it was common 'for the domestics of the families dealing with certain trades-people to demand from ten to twenty per cent discount (for their own pockets) on the amount of the quarterly, half-yearly, or yearly bills, when they (the servants) are sent with their masters cheque to discharge them'.

When the Prince spoke out against the practice, the following letter (faithfully reproduced) was received by a newspaper from a man worried that all tips might disappear:

I here the Prints of Wales has gone so fur as to say that even fees and prezzents of vales to suvvants is wrong, which is what to my mind aint zactly write. Shurely his Roil Ighness must have frogot Hisself. Taking bribes of a lot of low fellers like tradesmen, when a suvvant is sent to pay their bills, is certingly disgreysful on the part of any suvvant of onner; but when a noble party gives a gent's gentleman half-a-crown, which is the least to be ecspected of him, for anding im is at, is quite nother pair of shoes. With the pussentidges one's master is peckylated and defraudated. In the other, no one is out of pocket but the noble party hisself, which it is praps only a paltry half-crown which shurely aint mutch to fret Hisself about for the Hairy Parent.

I would not think that the Heir Apparent, or 'Hairy Parent', was too worried about the odd half-crown, so our anonymous correspondent need not have been so worried. In fact, the percentage system itself also continued in some quarters, for odd references to valets' discounts appear in Lobb account books as late as 1907.

John Lobb would have been less concerned about such minor irritants, than about his new expansion of the business in 1880. Then, and surely to the chagrin of Thomas's, he opened his second London premises at 29 St James's Street. Thomas and Son at number 36 was the only bootmakers in this famous street which now had jewellers, wine merchants, tailors, gun makers and booksellers catering for the needs of the members of the street's many clubs. In 1880, the street boasted White's, the Devonshire, the Verulam, the New University, the Cocoa Tree, Arthur's, the Conservative, the Thatched House, the United Eton and Harrow, and, next door to Lobb's new premises, Boodle's. Members of such august premises were unlikely to have been short of money and could easily combine a lunch or dinner with their order for a pair of boots, and John Lobb would naturally have been well aware of the fact before he took the new premises.

The manager he placed in charge of the new shop while he continued to oversee his shop and home at 296 Regent Street was the one-time apprentice and now master bootmaker Frederick Richards. Now thirty-two, the founder's brother-in-law, having suffered the exacting demands of his employer during his apprenticeship, was a poacher turned game-keeper *par excellence*. Autocratic, occasionally violent, and a stern disciplinarian, he ruled the St James's Street roost and woe betide any man who slacked or tried to cross him. Following in his master's footsteps, he relished a good drinking session, and when the party was over and he returned to the shop, his monumental hang-over needed a scapegoat for a therapeutic work-out.

Most often this took the form of rejecting any boots

brought in by an out-worker which were not up to his exacting standard. Many tales are told of Great Uncle Fred, who did not just reject an inferior pair of boots or an imperfect last, but chased the unfortunate offender to the door of the premises and hurled the last or the boots at his head. Richards, a bachelor, suffered from angina as a result of his life style and died in 1907. His end was as colourful as his life. With a glass in his hand, he stood in a Devonshire public-house singing at the top of his voice a ballad called *Then You'll Remember Me*, collapsed and died with those very words on his lips. And, so far as this book is concerned, he has had his wish fulfilled.

8

FAMILY MATTERS

THE BUSINESS that John Lobb had built from nothing to a
world-famous name in the bespoke trade, supported himself
and his pleasures, an army of outworkers, and inside staff
like Frederick Richards. It was also sufficiently prosperous,
though we have no figures, to support the Lobb family. The
four surviving children of John and Caroline Lobb at some
time or another were involved in the family firm and
dependent on it for a livelihood. In addition to the first-
born, young John Lobb, there were two girls, Caroline
Victoria and Mary Aline, both born in Australia like their
brother and brought by their mother to rejoin their father at
296 Regent Street, where another son, William Hunter, was
born soon afterwards.

Both of them helped out at either St James's Street or
Regent Street, both were attractive, and both had inherited
some of their father's pioneering spirit. This much we know
because they caused some talk by defying social conventions
to the extent of riding through the West End on the top of a
horse-drawn omnibus—an unheard-of activity for genteel
young gels who should have ridden demurely inside with
a chaperone.

Caroline Victoria was petite, lovable and had a streak of
the paternal fire hidden beneath her calm exterior. She
married a Thomas Brooks who ran a picture gallery dealing
in Victorian paintings, contemporary works as they were
then. Business in oils was often good, and Tom Brooks made
money very fast. Unfortunately, he spent it even faster. He

bought a large house at Kingsbury which was then still deep in the heart of the country, and lived the life of a country gentleman. He had coach, horses, trappings, servants and expensive furniture and a cellar as part of the existence to which he wanted to be accustomed: everything, in fact, except the consistent high income to go with it.

A spectacular row over the couple's affairs reached a climax when he swept one of a pair of large Venetian vases from the mantelpiece in the elegant drawing-room. Caroline Victoria calmly picked up the other one, saying, with panache, 'We won't need this one now, will we?' she dropped it amidst the fragments of the first. Game, set and match to Caroline Victoria.

Her unhappy marriage to Brooks came to an end when he died of *delirium tremens* induced by over-indulging himself in the contents of his cellar, with the result that she was left with a defunct picture business. The Lobb family came to the rescue. For a time they supplied financial backing for Caroline to continue the gallery alone, but it went further into debt as tastes changed, and eventually had to be closed. The result was that every Lobb wall was hung with the surplus Victorian canvasses and prints. They were the sole legacy of the sad career of Thomas Brooks.

Mary Aline, Caroline's sister, fared better in the matrimonial stakes. Her choice fell on a farmer's son from Elstree. Leonard Wilshin. He was a quiet retiring man, who tried out various business ventures including a greengrocery establishment at Covent Garden.

Of the two surviving sons, John Lobb the younger was something less than a chip off the old block. As the eldest son, he was duly apprenticed to the family firm at about twelve or fourteen and went through the process of learning last-making, closing, clicking and the like, as well as being groomed to succeed his paternal namesake as leader of the family business. Alas, the best-laid plans of mice, men and bootmakers ...

Not to put too fine a point on it, young John was caught

with his hand metaphorically in the till. At least, he was
found out by his father in this or some similar dishonesty.
The Regent Street premises must have trembled to the foundations that day when John Lobb Senior pronounced the
sentence: henceforward he had no son John, and the unfortunate who bore his name was duly expelled from firm
and family alike. He never forgave or repealed the verdict.
The rest of the family were forbidden to contact the errant
son, and John Lobb's will, read when he himself died in
1895, made no mention of the renegade.

If John Lobb Senior had had his way, young John would
have disappeared into oblivion. Actually, we know that he
married a chorus girl who in later life was shaped like a
cottage loaf and was known delightfully as Big Auntie.
They lived in a small house in Margate and he pottered
about in a small rowing-boat quite happily until the end of
his days in the 1920s. We know this because, however much
John Lobb Senior would have disapproved, family loyalty
prevented all connections being severed. In this case, the
younger brother, William Hunter, took over his brother's
position but made sure that some of the family profits found
their way into the pocket of the man William Hunter's
children knew as Wicked Uncle John. Like most wicked
uncles in real life, if not in stories, they loved him and his
homely wife, with the added relish owing to the fact that
he had once done Something Bad.

William Hunter Lobb born in the Regent Street premises
in 1870, had been educated at the Philological School not
far away in Marylebone, not a private school but one providing a sound basic public education by the standards of the
day. He was sufficiently academic to win prizes—beautiful
leather-bound books, with decorative gold blocking, but
with grim-sounding titles of a forbiddingly didactic character.

In 1881 he was given the arithmetic prize—Theodore
Alois Buckley's *The Great Cities of the Middle Ages*—and
the general subjects prize—Sir George Cox's Epoch of

Modern History—*The Crusades*. The next year's title was no more appetising. As a second form prize, the twelve-year-old was given *The Crown of Success* by A.L.O.E., a piece of flagrant moral propaganda in the disguise of a novel in which the characters are either virtues or sins personified or representatives of school subjects—Mr Learning, Miss Folly, Messrs Arithmetic and Mathematics being fairly typical. The next year's prize was the French one—*La Case de l'oncle Tom*, yes, *Uncle Tom's Cabin* in French. I doubt that anyone told William Hunter how singularly appropriate this was—his father's namesake from Cornwall, but no relation, had edited Josiah Henson's autobiography in 1876, Henson being the real-life model for the fictitious Uncle Tom.

If he read these auspicious titles, at least they did him no permanent harm, and he went into the firm to become, in the fullness of time, a master bootmaker in his own right. Better educated than his father, and a quieter more refined character in every way, William Hunter eventually became the new head of John Lobb's. The interim period between his father's death and his own succession was filled by the formidable Frederick Richards. When William did succeed, he was at some pains to put the old tyrant in charge at the St James's Street premises and to continue in his own quiet way at Regent Street. Whether this was to spare himself the embarrassment of ordering about an older man and his father's old drinking companion, or because he could not work in a building where the air might be filled with flying lasts and boots at any moment, we shall never know.

Flying lasts were not the only hazard at a shop in those days. It could have been argued with some accuracy by social reformers that shops were amongst the most hazardous industrial premises in the whole of Britain. From 1875 to 1907, there was a phenomenal growth of all kinds of shops and stores which increased in numbers from 295,000 up to 459,592 in the period. Probably upwards of a million people worked in the mushrooming retail outlets that many manufacturers opened up to accommodate their own and others' products. For example, William Timpson had started out in 1869 at about the same time as John Lobb, but by 1896 he had twenty-six shops and was producing 750 pairs of shoes a week. Oliver's from 1888 to 1892 were opening a branch every three weeks, and hundreds of other parallels could be cited.

In this twilight Kippsian world, long hours were worked, even the best class of shop not closing until 7 p.m. in the evenings and 6 p.m. on Saturdays, and assistants having to put up with unofficial overtime and deliveries for hours after the premises nominally closed. At best a 60-65 hour week was worked, but even 85 and 90 hours were common in the poorer class of shop. Although a House of Commons Committee had unanimously declared as early as 1886 that long hours were ruinous to health, and despite over 300 petitions asking for an enactment of an early closing bill, most of the unfortunate shopworkers had to work on regardless.

Tuberculosis, or consumption as it was termed, was rife. From 1900 to 1909, deaths from consumption were averaging 30 per cent of all deaths in shopworkers. And from 1905 to 1909, over 58 per cent of the deaths were caused by some kind of respiratory disease. If this sounds fairly frightening, it becomes even more so when we remember that the figures for *coal-mining* in the same periods were 14.3 per cent and 22.7 per cent respectively. A shop could be a dangerous place. In return for the advantage of multiple chain stores and the convenience of the customers, a hidden human price had to be paid for the goods.

The shopworker barely owned his own soul. This was the era of 'living-in', not just for domestic servants, but also for shop assistants. Some employers forbade their male staff to marry on pain of dismissal, and contemporary reports abound with injustices like fines for leaving food on the plates, fees for excessive visits to the lavatory, stoppages from wages for being unable to introduce at least two articles to

each customer who came in, and stores which made a profit
on employees' food. At Maples in 1897, 170 living-in assistants were deliberately excluded from the voting register as
if they did not exist.

The following notice from a drapers' would be funny but
for the tragic implications for the unfortunates who had to
follow its instructions:

Store must open promptly at 6 a.m. until 9 p.m. all the year round.
Store must be swept, counter, base shelves and showcases dusted.
Lamps trimmed, filled and chimney cleaned, pens made, doors and
windows opened.
A pail of water and scuttle of coal must be brought in by each
clerk before breakfast if there is time to do so and attend customers
who call.
Any employee who is in the habit of smoking Spanish cigars,
getting shaved at a barbers shop, going to dances, and other such
places of amusement will surely give his employer reason to be
suspicious of his integrity and alround honesty.
Each employee must pay not less than one guinea per year to the
church, and attend Sunday school every Sunday.
Men are given one evening a week for courting purposes and two
if they go to prayer meetings regularly.
After fourteen hours work spare time should be devoted to reading
good literature.

Living-in died hard in the West End. Debenham and Freebody and D. H. Evans abolished it in 1906, but Marshall and
Snelgrove did not do so until 1914 and, under the particular
influence of its reactionary and immaculate managing
director, W. A. Sergeant, John Lobb's old friends Peter
Robinson's did not do so until 1920.

The most spectacular tyrant of the West End however,
and a man after Frederick Richards' heart, would have been
John Lewis. In 1920 he was 84 and still firmly in charge
of his faculties and his establishment. Within the walls of
the building, his word was law. His outspokenness had
landed him in prison in 1903 when he slandered his own
ground landlord. His shop had looked like an election committee rooms when he plastered it with posters in support of

Asquith against the upstart Lloyd George. His employees found his activities less amusing.

If one of his van-boys let a customer get away with paying ¾d, ½d or ¼d short by cheque when goods were sent C.O.D., he stopped the money out of their wages. He signed an agreement allowing his employees to join a trade union then sacked every man who did and only re-employed them if they were prepared to sign a paper saying that they would not join. He even sacked one man who, by an enterprising campaign to rid the firm of water-damaged stock, earned more money on commission than Lewis thought he should have. With his white spade-shaped beard wagging vehemently up and down as he condemned the 'vapourings of the accursed Trade Unionists', he set the style for all too many an employer.

William Hunter Lobb had none of the John Lewis traits about him. Operating in a quieter manner than his own manager, his mildness sometimes led him astray. When he appointed a manager called Joyce to succeed the late Frederick Richards, the man who had been a life long friend proved to be dishonest and had to be discharged.

His next appointment proved a wiser choice: Thomas Moore, employed first by old John Lobb as a shop boy at St James's Street in 1883, was promoted to manager. It was a wise choice, for Moore remained a Lobb employee for 57 years.

With the end of the nineteenth century, we move into a period for which records are fairly complete so we can take a closer look at William Hunter Lobb, the Edwardian businessman, at home and at work, and at the other group who ensured the continuing success of Lobb's—the customers.

9

BOOTS FOR BOSIE

As MONDAY 31st December 1900 drew to a close, a new
century, our own, was being born. There was no clean break
with the past for 1901 was to be a year with harbingers of
the new fighting for attention with the old. Shaw's *Plays
for Puritans* looked to the future, Rudyard Kipling's *Kim*
to the past. Art Nouveau was flourishing, Frank Lloyd
Wright's new architectural ideas were breaking the ubiquitous stranglehold of the Victorian Gothic, and Queen
Victoria's own long reign came to an end. The strains of
Dvorak, Franck and Rachmaninov emanated from the concert platforms, Verdi died, Tenniel retired from *Punch*, and
that most typical of twentieth-century figures, Walt Disney,
was born.

From Australia, news was coming that Maclaren's
cricketers, flushed with a First Test victory by an innings
and 124 runs in the very last nineteenth century test, were
being skittled by Noble to lose the second of the series and
the twentieth century's first, by 229 runs.

In the London theatres, there was little indication that
a new age had dawned. Drury Lane had its traditional
pantomime; Beerbohm Tree, the manager of Her Majesty's,
was in the title role of Stephen Phillip's *Herod*; the St
James's Theatre under George Alexander had Mrs Craigie's
The Wisdom of the Wise; Julia Neilson was at the Globe;
Floradora ran and ran at the Lyric; Marie Tempest played
Nell Gwynn at the Prince of Wales; Charles Hawtrey played
at the Avenue; Frank Benson's company went through their

athletic paces in *The Merry Wives of Windsor* at the
Comedy; Ellaline Terris and Seymour Hicks at the Vaudeville played possibly the only *Alice in Wonderland* in
theatrical history where the Mad Hatter was married to
Alice; Gilbert and Sullivan's *Patience* had its umpteenth
performance at the Savoy; and Mrs Patrick Campbell was
managing the Royalty where she presented a play by Frank
Harris.

A case could be made out for William Hunter Lobb as
bootmaker to the theatrical profession. The account ledgers
covering the years from 1899 to 1906 shows that the numbers
of customers grew from 2,082 to 2,353 and that they included some of the most glittering names of the stage.

There was George Alexander, to be knighted in the
Coronation year of 1911, who managed the St James's
Theatre from 1891 until his death in 1918. Usually bow-tied
with his hair parted in the middle, this fine actor of all
parts calling for dignity and romantic charm was a frequent
visitor and a good customer. He had started his career as an
enthusiastic amateur, spent three years touring in Tom
Robertson's influential play *Caste*, and came to London in
1881 to join the great Henry Irving at the Lyceum. Spurred
by his acclaim as Faust, he blossomed into one of London's
most famous managers and under his auspices, the polite
mannered comedy of *Lady Windermere's Fan* and the
swashbuckling adventures of *The Prisoner of Zenda* drew
an audience as well-dressed and elegant as himself. For both
his stage appearances and his spare-time hobbies of riding,
golf, and driving, if not for fencing, he was content to be
shod by Lobb's.

Perhaps he introduced Charles Hawtrey to the firm, or
vice-versa. Hawtrey, the son of an Eton master but himself
educated at Rugby, was another customer who took an
inordinate pride in his appearance. His trim moustache with
never a hair out of place, his extravagant bonhomie well
known around the London scene, he was rarely in credit
to anyone but had sufficient charm to waive aside bills with-

out causing resentment, and could invariably quote a biblical text to cover any contingency. He charmed and— eventually—he paid. He had been launched to fame by his London production of *The Private Secretary* which achieved a phenomenal run, went on the American vaudeville circuit for five years and returned to England to write a three-act comedy, *Mr Martin*, and to become a Lobb customer.

And where Alexander and Hawtrey were shod, so were Mr and Mrs Hicks. Seymour Hicks was a fanatically active and versatile man. Known in later life as the Admirable Crichton on and off the stage, he had been the principal light comedian at George Edwardes's Gaiety from 1893 to 1898 until he too saw the lure of America. He was brought back by Charles Frohmann, the American entrepreneur, to the Vaudeville where he starred in J. M. Barrie's *Quality Street*, and also wrote plays and musicals himself; his good looks continued to draw audiences until the end of his long life. He died in 1949, having entertained troops in both World Wars and was knighted in 1935.

Mrs Seymour Hicks, as she appears in the Lobb ledgers, but Ellaline Terriss as we remember her, married her husband despite paternal disapproval, and shared in his triumphs in both *Quality Street* and his own *Blue Bell* as the striking light comedy actress-singer she always was. She even shared his bootmakers.

Lobb's cannot boast that they supplied Sir Henry Irving, unless his name appears in the older records now lost, but they can claim the next best thing in having supplied his eldest son H. B. Irving, (another Admirable Crichton), throughout his life. Having launched first into a career as a barrister, 'HB' was called to the bar in 1894 but never practised because he was then lured by the attraction of following in his father's footsteps. He had spells with Ben Greet on tour and with George Alexander at the St James's theatre. Curiously, Irving *fils* never lost his interest in the law for he wrote books on criminology and was an inveterate spectator at the Old Bailey's most sensational trials.

Not only was there an Irving on the books, there was also a representative of that other famous histrionic family (histrionic in both senses of the word), the Barrymores. Ethel Barrymore, at this time a tall, slim girl with beautiful doe-eyes that could send shivers up and down most male spines, was to become one of the leading women of the American stage, playing all the major classical roles such as Ophelia and Portia, and portraying Lady Teazle in her own Ethel Barrymore Theatre in New York in 1928. What is less often remembered is that she played with Irving in *The Bells*. Like her brother John, who married and divorced four times, she must have been something of a character.

One of Sir Henry Irving's *bêtes-noires* was a faithful Lobb customer. This was William Archer, the critic and author who had long championed modern plays: he edited and translated five volumes of Ibsen to make the texts readily available in English, collaborated with his friend Shaw, whose first play, *Widowers' Houses*, grew from an Archer play, and severely and rightly criticised Sir Henry for lending his major acting talents to unworthy melodramatic scripts like *The Bells*.

Another famous son of a famous father came into the shop from time to time. This was Dion Boucicault. Never the equal of the author of *The Coleen Bawn* and *London Assurance*, the son nevertheless managed both the Court Theatre and the Criterion and produced at the Duke of York's under Charles Frohmann.

There can be no doubt that Lobb's were known in Green Room circles. In the columns of *The Referee*, the sporting and literary paper, on November 8th 1903, the name of the firm is used in a satirical poem without explanation, so they must have been well-known enough amongst the readers for them to get the point. A Miss Pearl Mary Teresa Craigie had written in *The Daily Telegraph* a complaint regarding the attention-seeking behaviour of ladies at the theatre. She suggested that 'if women in the audience wish to excite more interest or attention than the players of the stage, they can

always pace the corridor of some crowded hotel'. 'L.G-T.'
of *The Referee* was worried that the offending ladies or
gents might take the hint:

The Drama erratic is 'off' the dramatic, and leans on dinner and
dress,
And the latter's a matter inviting the chatter of dramatists—more
or less.
And from one we hear that our ladies dear are wrong to favour the
stalls,
With dresses smart only meant for the Art of Dinner Parties and
Balls.
If they wish to excite admiration at night with shoulders, et
cetera, bare,
Our snug hotel corridors (barring the horrid doors) offer occasion
rare!
Oh, the heart it aches, and the brain it shakes, and the pitying soul
it sobs,
For our John Pearl Mary Teresa Craigie Oliver Hobbes!*

And the beautiful 'dreams' of our Pasquin, it seems, are for public
hotels alone,
Where the lift-gates click and the carpets are thick, and the air is
as cold as stone.
The theatre gown should be Quaker brown, of some sort of cloth
that's rough—
A serge, a tweed, or a frieze, indeed, would be perfectly good enough.
If gloves at all, they must not be a mall, but baggy and cotton-made,
Of the dull greyish green of the coffee bean, or a baked potato shade.
And perhaps the caps (to be worn in the laps) should be what are
described as 'mobs',
Now, really—John Pearl Mary Teresa Craigie Oliver Hobbes!

And the men at the periods when they are taking their wives to
the play?
Will anything do for shirt or shoe that is not in the evening way?
Must the chill hotel be their fate as well when attired in evening dress,
Where the one tongue hung among old and young is incessantly
on the guess?
To grace such a place as a theatre with lace is in women a foolish fad,
And the fellow who goes to theatrical shows in the swallow-tail
coat is mad.

* The best-selling author of the day, Mrs Pearl Craigie, used the pseudonym
'John Oliver Hobbes'.

He must save for the Brussels of 'Cecils' and 'Russells' the *tread of
  his patent Lobbs*—
So saith
    John
      Pearl
        Mary
          Teresa
            Craigie
              Oliver
                Hobbes!

However tedious the rhyme scheme and heavy-handed the
humour, it is interesting to see from the phrase I have
italicised how well Lobb's were known.

I must not give the impression that the theatre was the
only world walking on Lobb soles. With the one common
denominator being the fact that they could afford to patronise the town's top bootmaker, the sales ledgers are full of
minor royalty: for example, H.R.H. the Prince of Asturias
from Madrid; Eastern potentates such as Rajah Pudiekoto of
Madras and the Maharajah of Cooch Behar; peers of the
realm like Lord Inchiquin, Lord Tankerville and Lord
Sherbourne; forgotten European aristocrats yet to feel the
full draught of social change like Count Reventlow, Prince
Stanislaus Lubomirski and Prince Louis Esterhazy; rich
industrialists or merchants like the Rothschilds and the
Cunards and the Liebigs; and a number of others rather
more interesting than these in their own right.

There was Joseph Pulitzer, the Hungarian who had emi-
grated to the United States in 1864 and served in the Civil
War in the US cavalry. He became a congressman, but
resigned to concentrate on his growing newspaper empire
which was associated with many a political rumpus. He
supported Grover Cleveland for President, backed the steel
strikers in 1892, saw his aide shoot down a lawyer in a
political row at St Louis, and gave one million dollars to
found a school of journalism. He must have needed his
Lobb shoes to stand as firm as he did when the US government indicted him for criminal libels of Roosevelt and others

when he asked some searching questions into the distribu-
tion of the 40 million dollars from the French Panama
Canal Company in 1909; in the event, there was no prose-
cution. Known in the shop as a small bearded mild man with
pince-nez, spectacles perched on his nose with a cord
attached to them in case they fell, Pulitzer's name lives on
today in the prizes that he established for plays and other
literary works.

There was the newly established baron, Sir Henry
Stafford Northcote, who celebrated his appointments as the
Governor of Bombay in 1899, and Governor-General of
Australia in 1903, with new pairs of Lobb boots.

Among the other celebrities was Sir Martin Conway,
whose expeditions in the Himalayas, the Alps and the
Andes had brought him a gold medal for mountain surveys
at the Paris Exhibition in 1900, and left him with a taste
for good sound footwear that lasted him throughout his
later life as the first Director of the War Museum and a
Conservative member of parliament from 1918 to 1931.

A few pages away from Conway under the 'C's was Neville
Chamberlain, younger than Conway by fifteen years, neither
of them having the slightest idea that the young Chamberlain would one day be Prime Minister, and that the name
would become synonomous with appeasement.

The armed forces were represented by Colonel Sir Robert
Warburton, veteran campaigner in Abyssinia and the
Afghan War of 1879-80, who remained a customer until his
death in 1899; and among the naval officers were Admiral
Watson, who had been a midshipman in the China War of
1842, captained the famous *Temeraire*, and fought in the
Crimean war, and Admiral Palliser who was Commander-
in-Chief of the Pacific station from 1869-99 and remained a
keen sportsman till his death in 1907; these were just three
from many.

William Collins Whitney, the American who owned the
1901 Derby winner, Volodoyowski, and the one-time Lord
Mayor of London, Sir Sydney Waterlow, who gave up his

thirty-acre Highgate estate (which is called Waterlow Park after him) to the LCC, were both Lobb customers, but pride of place must surely go to the two men who follow—Lord Alfred Douglas and Frank Harris.

Lord Alfred's part in the Oscar Wilde tragedy and Frank Harris's emergence as the king of Pornographers in his autobiography *My Life and Loves* (only recently made generally available in this country) caused much whispering and scandal-mongering among their shocked Edwardian and late Victorian contemporaries.

History will probably be much kinder to Bosie and adjudge him more sinned against than sinning for his part in the triangle which finished Oscar Wilde, and may point more to the so-called faithful Robert Ross as the villain of the piece. That is something which must lie outside the scope of this book, but one would love to know if ever Bosie was in the shop at the same time as George Alexander who had obliterated Wilde's name from the bills outside his theatre and had refused Bosie's request to help raise bail for Wilde. It would have been a delicate situation for William Hunter Lobb if they were.

Whispers amongst the staff would have been inevitable when Frank Harris came in. A thick-set but short man with a dark jowl and complexion, Harris sported a large moustache and some less than discreet jewellery on his fingers and tie. He was an inveterate liar and gossip, and laid strong claims to being a reincarnation of Casanova in the gay nineties if his own accounts of his seductions and *affaires* can be believed, which sometimes they can. Under how many beds Harris's Lobb boots were left, the reader must calculate himself from Harris's memoirs.

Harris had, according to Max Beerbohm, 'a marvellous speaking voice, like the organ at Westminster Abbey, and with infallible footwork' (!) and another contemporary comment upon him came from Oscar Wilde, whose retort to a Harris account of how socially acceptable he had become was 'Yes, dear Frank, we believe you—you have dined in every house in London ...', and, after a pause, '... once!'.

Perhaps it would be of interest here to give details of Lord Alfred's and Frank Harris's dealings with Lobb's, both for the light they shed on the men themselves and also for what they tell us of prevailing prices. Here first are Frank Harris's purchases at Lobb's from 1899 to 1902, year by year:

1899

July 4th	1 pair of Russian Leather laced boots	£2	18	0d
	Plus case		1	0d
July 17th	1 pair Calf leather shoes with toecaps	£2	14	0d
	Plus case		1	0d
	Plus balance from previous ledger	£3	12	3d
		£9	6	3d
Oct 5th	1 pair Calf boots with toecaps stout	£2	18	0d
	Case		1	0d
Dec 9th	1 pair Patent Black no caps	£2	16	0d
	Case		1	0d
		£15	2	3d

1900

Feb 12th	1 pair Russia Leather with caps	£2	18	0d
	1 High Leg Golosh Kid, Brogue caps	£2	7	6d
Feb 26th	1 High Leg Russia Leather with caps	£2	15	0d
	Post			6d
		£23	3	3d
Oct 16th	Russia with caps	£2	18	0d
	Carriage and post		1	6d
Dec 14th	Calf with lace and caps	£2	14	0d
	Patent leather Buttoned	£2	16	0d
	Case		1	6d
Dec 22nd	1 Pair of boots soled and heeled		10	6d
	Post			6d

1901

March 6th	1 pair Calf Leather boots with caps	£2	14	0d
	1 pair boot trees	£1	18	0d
	Carriage			2d

April 10th	1 pair Calf Boots no caps	£2 18 0d
June 12th	1 pair Russia Leather soled and heeled	12 6d
	1 pair brown laces	1 0d
		£40 8 11d

1902

Aug 15th	1 pair White canvas and Russia Leather Oxford style	£2 12 6d
Sept 16th	1 pair Russia Leather with caps	£2 18 0d
Dec 3rd	1 pair Calf leather with caps	£2 14 0d
Dec 20th	2 pair Buck Oxford style with caps	£2 12 6d
	1 pair Russia leather with caps	£2 15 0d
	Post	6d
		£54 1 5d

It appears from this that Harris was able to run up over
the course of at least five years a bill of over fifty pounds,
towards which he actually paid £20 in August 1902 and
another £20 in October 1902; like many other men about
town, he was only able to look his best because of the long
term credit he was allowed. The number of pairs he bought
is about average for the time, although other customers
bought three and four times as many, thus this account may
be taken as a good indication of the expenses of an Edwardian gentleman. Moreover, it shows to what extent
Disraeli's famous definition of England being two nations
was still overwhelmingly true. In the days when Harris was
going into Lobb's to buy two pairs of shoes at a time and
spending over five pounds, five pounds was more than the
average working man could expect to earn in a month.
Seebohm Rowntree, whose investigations into the lives of
the poor are well known, recorded an actual and typical
account of a labourer's expenditure on clothes:— a new
pair of boots, 11s; 4 pairs of socks at 9d each; a second-hand
coat, 4s; a pair of trousers, 7s 6d; a second-hand overcoat
which had to last 3 years, 15s; 3 shirts, 1s 4d each; and a
cap and scarf, 1s 7d; total, £2 6s 1d. In other words Harris

was paying more for one pair of shoes than many thousands of people were able to spend on an entire wardrobe in a *year*.

This was not just a British phenomenon. Another famous Lobb customer, Andrew Carnegie, having set the pace in the American steel industry, was enjoying the Gay Nineties on an income of 23,000,000 dollars and more without having to pay taxes on a cent of it, while a majority of Americans were unable even to enjoy the luxury of an inside toilet.

Lord Alfred Douglas though shown on the ledgers to be a model customer, certainly knew some poverty during his life; it is known that in his days in Paris at the end of the nineties he was forced to be beholden to his landlady for everything from clothes to cigars. His life was far from happy: an elopement resulted in a short-lived marriage; at only thirty, in 1900 his beauty was already in decline; and there was continued bitterness between him and Ross. Nevertheless he bought and he paid as the following extract shows:

1899					1899				
Brought forward	£29	3	3d		Dec 9 By cheque	£10	0	0d	
1900					**1900**				
					Feb 16 By cheque	£19	3	3d	
Oct 20 2 pairs Calf	£5	8	0d		Oct 20 Cash	£5	8	0d	
1902					**1902**				
					June 12 Cheque	£7	2	6d	
June 30 1 pr Russia	£2	18	0d						
1 pr Calf Button boots	£2	14	0d						
July 28 1 pr Russia, caps	£2	18	0d		July 28 do	£4	1	6d	
1 pr Calf Button boots	£2	14	0d						
	£11	4	0d			£11	4	0d	
Aug 16 1 pr Patent Oxford no caps	£2	2	0d		Aug 16 Cash	£2	2	0d	

There can be no doubt that although Bosie was not welcome in many a London club, William Hunter Lobb must always have been glad to see him, and it was thanks more to the Bosies of the world who paid, rather than the Harrises who did not, that William Hunter Lobb could claim that he was a successful Edwardian businessman. In 1901 he had two premises, the one at 296 Regent Street where he sold shoes to the value of £4,739 and made a net profit of £234, in addition to his salary, and the one at 55 St James's Street where the sales totalled £9,210 and the net profit was £2,026, with the additional profit of £36 4s 6d made by selling seats in the shop to those who wished to see Queen Victoria's funeral procession from a good vantage-point. (In 1902 the same seats for Edward's Coronation made another welcome £34 4s 9½d.)

It is apparent that the opening of the St James's Street establishment by old John Lobb had been no idle speculation but a move demonstrating considerable business acumen, on which much of William Hunter's prosperity depended.

William Hunter Lobb had himself expanded the business by opening a branch at 1 Rue du Vingt Neuf Juillet in Paris in 1901, but he must surely have wondered initially if his enterprise in the foreign capital was a mistake. In Paris in the first year he sold a modest £1,341 worth of boots and shoes and made a net loss of £274. In the next three years, the Paris shop made losses of £100, £134 and £168 respectively, and the tide did not turn in his favour until 1904 when a modest profit of £157 showed that perhaps the idea had been a good one after all. It continued to be, and by 1913 the profits had grown to £1,398—a very slight setback from the £1,497 of 1912. The sales of 1913 totalled £10,585, confirming his expectations that there would indeed be a demand in Paris for Lobb shoes.

He was very much a man of ideas, for he was awarded a Patent in May 1906 for a solution which included such unlikely ingredients as spirit black and vinegar, for polishing wax on the flesh side of calf with a cream polish once the solution has been applied to the skin.

His attempted expansion in London was less successful. In the next few years, sales and profits in Regent Street were always well below those at St James's Street. Undeterred, or perhaps thinking that Regent Street had more possibilities than were readily apparent, in 1904 he added more premises at 292 Regent Street, next door but one to the other one. Both shops were in Regent Street in the block between Margaret Street and Great Castle Street.

Unfortunately, the new shop did not enhance the possibilities of its neighbour. Rather it became a millstone around its neck. Although number 292 made a modest profit in 1905 of £80, it went rapidly downhill, losing £162 in 1906 and £301 in 1907; the latter was particularly alarming because St James's Street made only £232 profit and number 296 only £159 in that year!

1907 was also the year that Lobb reached an agreement with the London and Provincial Union of Hand-sewn Boot and Shoe Makers on a list of new prices for work. A copy of the list is still extant, and shows in detail a piece-worker's rates of pay (*see* illustration).

The new rates were only part of his 1907 problems. Faced with the loss at 292 Regent Street, Lobb was aware that something had to be done. Not unnaturally, his firm of accountants, who had prepared his balances since 1902, recommended that he sell number 292 as rapidly as he could. He took the advice eventually but not quickly enough. In 1908, before he found a taker for the property, 292 Regent Street had lost him £1,457. And there was precious comfort at his other premises; number 296 and St James's Street, for once included in a joint balance sheet, sold £16,660 worth, but lost £80 on the year's dealings. He must have been very pleased with his Paris venture for that brought in profits of £785 to offset the London losses.

Sensibly, he rationalised the situation, disposed of both the Regent Street premises and was rewarded with £1,598 profits at St James's Street within twelve months i.e. in 1909. From then on, he settled to a stable and indeed profitable existence. 1913 would be a fairly representative year.

In that year salaries, including Lobb's own, came to £1,533, and wages to inside and outside staff £6,459. He had to write off £511 to bad debts, £773 to stock, £373 to 'rates and taxes', £250 to post and carriage, £5,736 to buying materials etc., and £782 to rent. He sold £19,456 worth of boots and shoes and made a gross profit of £6,780, leaving a net profit of £2,040 to add to his capital account. The latter had accumulated by 1913 to £10,934. William Hunter Lobb was no Andrew Carnegie, but these figures suggest that he may have been something of a middle range Forsyte, and it was of the Forsytes one might be reminded when considering the sort of life he led outside his business.

10

WAR AND PROFITS

BEFORE THE changes in business premises had occupied his attention, William Hunter Lobb had undertaken some private house-hunting. His choice finally settled on North West London, where he took a large house in St John's Wood at 105 Alexandra Road. Improved transport facilities had made St John's Wood a growing and fashionable suburb ideally placed for the City and West End business-man.

One event in his private life which had precipitated the decision was his marriage. On January 14th 1901, he walked up the aisle of St James's Church Piccadilly to be wed to Betsy Smerdon, a woman almost two years older than himself although that was kept a closely guarded secret for years afterwards.

She was a farmer's daughter, born at Forder Farm in South Brent, Devonshire, on 15th November 1868. She was no gauche country girl, unwise in the ways of the world, for she had come to London in her twenties and had worked for her living. She was thirty-two when she married and had matured to a strong but lovable character.

She would have been well aware of the many social injustices and inequalities in the shops of London for she had worked in the house-keeping department of John Barker's at a time when, as we have seen, employees 'lived in' on the premises. She must have been very competent for she went from there to the Mandeville Hotel in Mandeville Place to become the manageress of all the domestic staff.

How and where she met William we do not know, but obviously she was sufficiently attracted by the smartly-dressed businessman (from contemporary photographs it is clear that he was a handsome man) to give up her independence. Their honeymoon was typical—a Grand European Tour.

All the indications are that this was a happy match. She brought her competence to bear in providing a well-ordered household for the bread-winner's return home each day, and he continued to prosper.

The first son was born in November 1901 and was christened John Hunter Lobb. He would have been the obvious successor to his father's business in the years to come, but tragically he died in infancy of pneumonia. More happily, the next son, William, born in 1902, was sturdy and he was followed by Victor in April 1905 and Eric in March 1907. These three healthy boys grew up in an atmosphere of love, security and comfort.

On a typical day in the Lobb household, the master would rise to open his mail and eat a hearty breakfast prepared by the servants; domestic or family matters would be discussed over the breakfast table while a nanny looked after the children. Mrs Lobb would issue the household orders of the day to the staff a little later, having discussed any points of difficulty with her husband before he left for business. At the appointed hour, Invest the coachman would arrive outside in the brougham drawn by a big bay horse, Duke, to drive him from St John's Wood down to St James's Street. Invest had come around from the Maida Vale mews where the horses, the brougham and other vehicles were kept for the family's convenience.

The coachman in his full livery intrigued the young Lobb children partly because they had overheard that he fed his many rabbits on oats which should have gone to the horses, and partly because he was supposed to be able to decapitate sparrows with his whip. Whenever they themselves had been out with him, either he had been feeling

Bootmakers away from the last. (*Left*) Old John Lobb leans on his walking stick, in the company of unidentified friends. (*Below*) William Hunter Lobb (second row, fifth from the left) surrounded by his employees at a 1900 firm's 'beanfeast' outing to Taplow, Berkshire

Outworkers from two centuries: (*above*) a Victorian
bootmaker, and (*below*) Geoff Kane, one of Lobb's
present outworkers in his Devonshire workshop

well-disposed towards sparrows or the word had gone
around the feathered kingdom and there had been no more
recruits to the kamikaze sparrows squadron. Nevertheless,
the dark possibility was still there and they would watch
Invest with awe.

Their father in top hat, frock coat and buttoned boots
would bid them farewell and climb in behind Invest to bowl
along to town. At about 6.30 in the evening he would return,
another day's bootmaking business completed, change into a
smoking jacket and sit by his smoking cabinet, which con-
tained a large selection of pipes and a bowl of his own special
mixture of tobacco, until dinner was ready. Before the couple
sat down to the meal, the children, washed, pink and shining
were brought in by nanny to say goodnight before being
tucked up in bed.

At children's parties or on special occasions, this gentle
and perhaps basically shy man would be persuaded to stand
beside the piano and run through his repertoire of Victorian
drawing-room ballads sung in a discreet and pleasing light
baritone.

The costs of living in such congenial circumstances compared with today's were infinitesimal, but should be seen in
the perspective of the figures already given for a poor man's
clothing budget. Coal for heating and cooking was £2-3 a
quarter, rent was £17 10s od a quarter, rates £9 a year,
water £1 10s od a year and the servants' wages (for coachman, parlourmaid, cook, nanny and gardener) £5 a month.
For one of those servants on 5s a week, such bills would
have been astronomical.

Mrs Lobb did much of her shopping at William
Whiteley's in Queens Road and though the following may
not be totally representative so far as purchases are concerned, they give a nice picture of prices and customs in
the Edwardian era. In October 1912, she was billed by the
shop for the following supplies:

To A/c rendered		7s	5d
Amazon Parrot	£2	2	od
& Perch		1	8d
Canary		7	6d
Seed			5d
Sand			4½d
1 repeater alarm clock		6	6d
1 cage		7	9d
Iron shoe			10½d
Fox terrier puppy		15	od
1 dog basket		3	11d
Squirrel stole	£3	9	6d
Squirrel muff	£3	3	od
	£11	5	11d
Dust bin		9	9d
Bread jar		9	6d
	£12	5	2d

In May 1914, the services of Whiteley's were called in for a dinner party given by the couple. The bill ran as follows:

6 stalks Hollyhock @ 2 11d		17	6d
6 sprays Lilac @ 8¾d		4	4½d
To services of one chef, including interviews and fares	£1	5	od
Services of Man to carve till 11.30 p.m.		8	6d
Services of Waitress 4 p.m. till 11.30 p.m.		8	6d
Services of Man & Waitress for the extra hour 11.30 p.m. till 12.30 a.m.		4	od
Cab fares returning at 12.30 a.m.		2	od
12 fish knives and forks		2	6d
Packing and removing dinner service		10	od
Insurance in transit		6	6d
	£4	8	10½d

Is it not revealing of the times that two people should be hired for the best part of eight hours for less than it cost for six stalks of flowers?

William Hunter Lobb liked the open air and the country as well as the comfort of the town or perhaps he liked sometimes to escape from the noisy menagerie. He rode on Hampstead Heath, went clay-pigeon shooting, and he and his wife took holidays down on her family's farm in Devon. Another family custom, if not practically an institution, was the annual holiday at Margate.

This was an expedition in the nature of a mass exodus. A furnished house was booked at Cliftonville, near Margate, and growlers hired from a West London firm called to collect the large, noisy party of adults, children, canaries, parrots, dogs and servants that was to be taken to Victoria station. When the party disgorged itself from the growlers at the station, one or more distant cousins, unable on their own devices to afford a summer holiday turned up nominally to see the family off until William Hunter, with the suggestion of a twinkle in his eye, would ask gravely, 'I don't suppose you'd like to come, would you?' and the delighted cousin or cousins, grinning happily, would be parked somewhere in the middle of the quarrelling, laughing, singing, barking, squawking, chirping party on their way to Margate Station. Once there, competition broke out for the honour of being the first person to ride along the front in the goat-chaise, although there would be two whole glorious months of opportunity for the trip, as there would be for the obligatory visit to the wild animals and the circus of the Hall by the Sea (now called 'Dreamland').

The expedition was also a reunion. Wicked Uncle John who had done Something Bad and the cottage loaf Big Auntie would be at the station welcoming the brother and his family, as company for themselves and their children, however much old John Lobb would have disapproved of the situation and the mutual family affection.

*   *   *

This was the Edwardian era, the last Indian summer of prosperity before the First World War came to put an end to the cosy existence enjoyed by so many. For the Lobb family, there was, after the outbreak of war in 1914, another grave blow to face, and though they might have ridden the former, the latter had far-reaching effects on their life-style. Almost before they became really aware of the economic effects of the war on civilian life, William Hunter Lobb, who had been in decline from illness for at least two previous years, died from empyema in 1916.

So far as the business was concerned, there was no Lobb who could take over and follow on the succession of old John and William Hunter and, more seriously, so far as the family was concerned, it left Betsy Lobb without a husband and with three growing boys to be educated without a father to support them. To a certain extent, William Hunter had ensured them a future for he had left money in trust for them for their coming of age. In the meantime, Betsy Lobb was left as the sole proprietor of a business she knew nothing about, and the head of a town establishment beyond her new circumstances. She needed all her inner resourcefulness to take quick and momentous decisions.

It is a tribute to her character that every decision appears in retrospect to have been thoroughly sound. In common with many good parents, her first consideration was that her sons should continue to have the best education she could give them. For a while they were able to continue at their schools in London, but this unfortunately came to an end; not because of the expense but because of the Kaiser. One of the Kaiser's representatives floating over St John's Wood in a Zeppelin dropped a bomb which exploded at the back of the house. It did no more than slightly shock the occupants and break the panes in the kitchen window, but it was enough for Betsy Lobb. Certainly not from fear, but from the sensible calculation that there was little point in educating her boys only to see them blown up, she decided to take them away from London.

By now, the Kaiser was having his indirect effect on the business. In Paris, there were weightier things on people's minds than whether they would be able to wait for a pair of hand-made boots to be ready. The healthy sales of £10,585 of 1913 had plummeted to £4,084 by 1915, and the welcome profit of £1,398 had turned into an alarming loss of £1,283; to this was added a loss of £408 even at home, as what seemed the entire male population headed for the Western Front to give their lives in ferocious struggles over perhaps a few yards of mud.

With these new financial demands upon him, William Hunter had been forced to dig into his capital account to balance the books, so Betsy Lobb took over £7,496, rather than the £10,000 or more she would have had but for the war. This brought her to another decision. Instead of seeing her capital and the future of the firm and family eroded, she decided that there had to be economies in living expenses instead.

Instead of the luxury of St John's Wood with servants and horses and the freedom to roam around a big garden and to keep a multitude of pets, the children had to reconcile themselves to the restrictions and the lack of privacy of furnished basement rooms in Brighton. They also had the grisly experience of finding a dead body washed up on the beach.

Naturally, they hated it. Probably Betsy Lobb hated it as much as they did, but at least she had the knowledge that the sacrifices in living standards meant that the boys could all attend Brighton College, and were being prepared for a better future. She had to get them away from the bombs, and she was giving John Lobb's Bootmakers a chance to survive through difficult times without further inroads being made into the carefully accumulated capital.

At Alexandra Road, her two sisters-in-law moved in with their families, her elegant furniture was piled into the one-time drawing room, the house was crowded with people and children and the beautifully kept garden dug up and planted

in the manner urgently recommended to everyone by Mr
Lloyd George. Some in Brighton, some in London, that was
the way the Lobb family saw out the war. The present
proprietor, Eric Lobb, has frankly admitted that he hated
every moment of every day of two world wars.

The eldest son William, who became known in the firm
inevitably as young Mr Will and later as Mr Will, was
always destined to take over the business in its third generation of Lobbs, but Betsy Lobb kept him at school until he
had completed his secondary education.

Starting at University College School, Hampstead, he had
spent the wartime years at Brighton College, but returned
to his old school at Hampstead when London was restored
to safety. He left school at sixteen to enter the firm and to
learn the full gamut of last-making, closing and making at
first hand from the Lobb workmen, supplemented by a
course at the Cordwainers' College in East London where
the theory and practice of bootmaking was taught in a
successful attempt to provide a continuity of craftsmanship
between the succeeding generations. This institution was
increasingly necessary for gradually the old-style father-to-
son tradition was dying out with the increased reliance on
machines.

Young Mr Will took to each new skill with enthusiasm,
and although he never progressed beyond confirming his
hatred of book-keeping and accountancy in the months he
spent with the firm's accountant, he found last-making ideally
suited to his temperament and taste. To the end of his
life, he could always find solace in times of difficulty by
going back to last-making and turning out a beautiful last
from an ungainly block of wood. That he was also a very
competent chess-player is another clue to his retiring, con-
templative nature. Another part of his Lobb education was
a seven-year spell in the Paris shop where again he found
ample opportunity to perfect his last-making.

Grooming a successor was all very well, but no sixteen-
year-old could have been expected to pick up the reins of

controlling the firm, so a manager had to be appointed in the interim. The choice fell on a man who had been appointed as a shop-boy at St James's Street by old John Lobb himself. On the death of William Hunter Lobb in 1916, Tom Moore, who had, so to speak, come up through the ranks, became the manager.

Tom Moore was not in the same mould of retiring, gentle handlers of men like William Hunter and his son Will; rather he was a throw-back to the John Lobb-Frederick Richards school. And if they had been commanding officers, he was the sergeant major. What he lacked in physical weight, he made up for in sternness. Pince-nez spectacles perched on his nose, thinning hair brushed back, his fierce expression reduced underlings to the status of Bob Cratchit, and they were very firmly put down if they ever got ideas above their lowly station. So far as he was concerned, that went for the Lobb family too.

As well as strictness he possessed moral uprightness and strong integrity. He upheld the standards of the craft and the reputation of the firm, made outworkers tremble if they dared to put a stitch out of place, and ensured with the firm's accountant, John Lake (whose brother Percy managed the Paris shop), and Ernest Sandford, the cashier, that there could be no repetition of the dishonesties of the past.

Although Betsy Lobb, as an absentee proprietor must have been vulnerable to deceit, thanks to these men and an exceedingly loyal staff who took all Tom Moore could throw at them without rebelling or taking their skill elsewhere, she received her full share of profits as the firm weathered the storm and moved into a new era of prosperity. She was supported by these men throughout the period of financial difficulty resulting from widowhood, and she succeeded in obtaining relief from recruitment (to the services) for the staff, which ensured the firm's survival for the rest of the war years.

The workmen were not lacking in ingenuity and resource-fulness themselves in times of shortage. Jim Saunders recalls that, during the First World War, the hog's bristles used for guiding the waxed thread through the holes punched by the awl in hand-sewing became well nigh impossible to obtain. At the pub in Berners Street, there was a conference at which one man came up with an ingenious idea.

It was adopted and a war party set out. Six noble boot-makers, armed with apples, pears and nuts set out, not for the Western Front but for Regent's Park and London Zoo. With an air of assumed casualness, the party wandered past various cages until there was no keeper in sight. When the coast was clear they converged on the hog enclosures. Two hogs were lured to the bars by the apples and pears and a selection of sweet hog-like noises. When the poor beasts lurched over, twelve hands suddenly descended and grabbed a handful of hair each. By the time the squeals had subsided, the party was in Regent's Park Road and on their way back to town with a six-month supply of bristles for the West End trade. Such bristles are used to this day.

11

KINGS AND UNCOMMONERS

THE TRADITION of supplying Lobb boots to the theatre world
was continued from the early years of the century through
to the post-war period. Men like George Alexander, now
Sir George Alexander, continued to patronise Lobb's and
one of his actors, A. E. Matthews, later the subject of many
an anecdote recalling his absent-mindedness and outrageous
adlibbing, had a Lobb man to visit the St James's Theatre to
fit him with dress boots for the play in which he was
appearing.

(A favourite A. E. Matthews anecdote is the story
related by his colleagues in a long-running play, who became exasperated by his maddening habit of introducing
fresh lines and business, and plotted with the stage manager
to sabotage him in turn. When Matthews sank into an armchair, the stage manager 'rang' the telephone on the occasional table by his side. Matthews picked it up, held the
receiver to his ear, then held it out towards the heroine and
said, 'It's for you!')

The Lobb man was Charlie Moore, the younger brother of
Tom Moore the manager, and it was Charlie who came on
television as 'a voice from the past' for A. E. Matthews when
Matthews was the subject of the television programme *This
is Your Life*.

In 1912, Pinero's farcical romance in three acts, *The
Amazons*, starring Weedon Grossmith, co-author with his
brother George of the memorable misadventures of Mr
Pooter in *Diary of a Nobody* and a specialist in playing

Pooter-style roles, Godfrey Tearle, Dion Boucicault and a very young Duncan Macrae, was revived at the Duke of York's theatre. It had the added distinction of Marie Lohr, Pauline Chase, Ruth Mackay and Phyllis Neilson-Terry all clad in riding-boots, and all duly fitted by Lobb's. The footwear was of rather more distinction than the play which was hardly the Arthur Wing Pinero's masterpiece (*The Second Mrs Tanqueray* and *Trelawney of the Wells* were written later than *The Amazons*) which he may well have realised, being a Lobb customer himself.

Two other authors of the day, Bernard Shaw and Rudyard Kipling, so far as may be firmly established, were never Lobb customers which seems rather surprising in view of the fact that their wives were faithful and long-standing customers.

Lobb's list of customers, numbering 3,099 by 1914, included representatives from the musical stage. The young conductor Thomas Beecham, who in 1910 had given his first opera season at Covent Garden, introducing the best from abroad with the English premiere of Strauss's *Elektra*, and performing English works among them Ethel Smyth's *The Wreckers* and Delius's *A Village Romeo and Juliet*, also made his appearance at the shop.

Lobb's attracted other musical talents who, earning huge fees for personal appearances and for the new gramophone recordings, were prepared to invest some of their earnings in superior footwear. The first of these was Enrico Caruso, one of the finest tenors of all time. When he first became a customer (and he continued as one for many years) his voice was at its best and his musicianship impeccable. When we remember that he was the first to become a famous recorded voice and that he earned between four and five hundred thousand pounds for his royalties on recordings alone, we can well understand that he could afford at least two pairs of Lobb shoes every time he visited London.

Yet, despite these huge earnings for every time he exercised his larynx, Caruso was prepared to give some recitals free. On one visit to the St James's Street shop, he held the staff spell-bound with an unaccompanied aria while he waited for his purchases to be wrapped. It was probably the smallest London audience ever to hear the golden voice, but they duly applauded him all the way to the door so they made up in warmth anything they may have lacked in numbers.

Another client was an obscure Russian shoemaker, who in 1913, needed a boot which reached about 12½ in conventional sizes and allowed for enlarged joints, abnormally curved heels and fallen arches. He is not remembered as a shoemaker, for that was the trade he gave up as a youth to become one of the world's greatest singing actors with a rich bass voice so sonorous that many would have sworn the sound emitted from the depths of his Lobb boots. Feodor Chaliapin, for such was he, although both the account books and the newspapers of the day uncertainly settled for Chaliapine*, was making his London debut at the Theatre Royal, Drury Lane and taking audiences by storm with his portrayal of Boris Godunov.

Unlike Caruso, he never gave a free performance for the Lobb workmen, but he remained a long-standing customer so the boots must have been to his satisfaction.

Whether the Lobb standards of service were being talked of in operatic circles or not, one other golden voice of the age can be added to the list. This was 'Count' John McCormack, the Dublin tenor whose uncanny phrasing, breath control and purity of tone ravished the ears of so many. He was never an actor of the Chaliapin standard, a fact he freely admitted, but after he gave up opera in 1913 his concert career knew no bounds. He became a Lobb customer shortly after his Covent Garden debut as Turiddu in *Cavalleria Rusticana* when, for the first time in his short life

---

* Italians I know are notorious for regarding all foreigners as non-singers, particularly in opera, but there can be little excuse for an article on Lobb's in the fashion magazine, *L'Uomo Vogue*, which solemnly assured us that one of the most famous of Lobb's customers was, and I quote, 'Shelly Apin (cantante russo)'.

(he was still only 23), he could afford such luxuries.

Lobb's also supplied men from vastly different walks of life, whose special talents had brought them to unaccustomed riches, among them Brownie Carslake, the superb jockey who won the St Leger three times; they also continued to supply those whose fortunes came by dint of their birth and social position.

One such was His Serene Highness Prince Louis Alexander of Battenburg who became, during his distinguished naval career, First Sea Lord from 1912 to 1914, and at the request of King George V a naturalised British subject when his German ancestry became an embarrassment during the war. Others included Prince Albert, later King of Belgium, and Prince Nicolas of Greece.

Most important of all, after the death of the first royal patron, King Edward VII, formerly Prince of Wales, his second son succeeded his father both to the throne in 1910 and to his bootmakers. This was King George V who, though never a trend-setter like his father, always insisted, rather delightfully on having his trouser legs creased at the sides and not down the front and back. That was perhaps the one eccentricity he ever permitted himself, for he was ever the model of constitutional rectitude and conservative respectability, virtues that stood him in excellent stead in the General Strike in 1926 when he was the one man in a position of authority to advocate restraint on both sides.

In the period of 1914-20, the Lobb boot became less a trademark of the statesman and the stage than a symbol of literary London. The ledgers of the period suggest that many royalties accruing to the writers of the day were converted in their turn to Lobb footwear.

Publishers like Jonathan Cape, and the American proprietor Condé Nast are mentioned here alongside Edward Knoblock, an American playwright born in New York in 1874 who became a naturalised British subject in 1916 so that he could serve in the British forces. Before he went off to war, he lived in Albany, so a call at Lobb's was never very inconvenient. He is probably best remembered today for his collaborations with Arnold Bennett, a fellow Lobb customer.

Another, Gerald Hamilton, became better known as the model for Christopher Isherwood's creation Mr Norris. Isherwood's readers will remember the care and attention which Norris lavished on Anni's long black boots!

Other writers who achieved great popular success if not perhaps comparable literary stature, were Frank Swinnerton, setting out on a very long career, and A. E. W. Mason. Mason, a strong healthy man who relished mountain-climbing and sailing, had twin careers as a Liberal Member of Parliament for Coventry from 1906 to 1910 as one of the many Liberals swept into office in the 1906 landslide victory, and as a writer whose work, *The Four Feathers*, first appeared in 1902 and provided through edition after edition perhaps the definitive account of attitudes to patriotism, and the popular ideal that man's duty was to fight for his country and his honour.

Less generally well-known, though of higher literary stature altogether, were two other customers, Ronald Firbank and Bernard Berenson. Firbank, a curious, wealthy and homosexual Roman Catholic, patronised the Junior Carlton and the Junior Constitutional clubs between his visits to Lobb's, although his brittle mannered prose with its decadent overtones of the *fin de siècle* is unlikely to have found a large readership in any of those establishments. Be that as it may, his bizarre taste never moved beyond the conventional when it came to boots and shoes, which being Lobb's, were as aesthetically pleasing as they were functional. They must have been to please Berenson. That so distinguished an art scholar and writer on aesthetics should be a customer is a triumphant vindication of the prevailing taste in the firm, at least with regard to style, material and colour.

Such matters would have been of some interest too to Marcus Stone who became a Royal Academician in 1887 after his father Frank Stone, and set some sort of record by winning international medals at Paris, Berlin, Vienna,

Philadelphia and Chicago even though he rarely showed his work outside the Royal Academy itself. There he exhibited his life studies and historical paintings in a phenomenal series of sixty-two consecutive exhibitions. He became a Lobb customer when he lived in Kensington. He often exchanged his brush for a billiard cue for he was extraordinarily keen on the game. Perhaps he was responsible for introducing a fellow Royal Academician to Lobb's, Sir William Newenham Montagu Orpen, a brilliant if mannered, painter, who belonged to a multitude of London clubs, from the Athenaeum to the Chelsea Arts, and in 1918 gave many of his war pictures to the nation.

Another famous customer was an American who had trained at the French Officers' School at Fontainebleau. He lived in a luxurious apartment in Paris laying the foundations of his subsequent reputation as one of Europe's and America's wealthiest playboys. He was a Lobb customer before the 'twenties, but it was during the 'twenties that he became the nonconformist sophisticate whose wit and sybaritic tastes epitomize that decade. This was Cole Porter, whose conspicuous wealth bought him not only hand-made shoes, but a life-style reminiscent of a Scott Fitzgerald character. Not even many Lobb customers could have run up the bills that Porter paid for events like the private party entertained by the entire Monte Carlo Ballet, or another at which all the guests were whisked off to the Riviera by motorcade on a sudden impulse. In 1923, he and his wife took over the Venetian palace where Browning had died, hired fifty gondoliers as footmen, and constructed a floating night club with a French chef, a negro jazz band and space for a hundred guests. And this, let it be noted, was at a time when hunger marchers were entering London to plead for a bare subsistence.

Wealth beyond most people's wildest dreams also distinguished other customers, for instance, Bernard Oppenheimer, leader of some five South African Diamond Corporations, and His Highness Maharajah Gaekwar Baroda Sir

Sayaji Rao III. From the resources of his territory of eight thousand square miles and two and a half million souls, the Maharajah was able to send to Britain and the allies during the war 500,000 rupees for aeroplanes, the same for the War Gift Fund, another 470,000 rupees for various War Relief funds, 1,500,000 rupees for the purchase of Ford vans, and a regular 12,000 rupees every month from January 1916 to the end of the War, plus 154 horses, thirteen tents and £5,000 to the Viceroy's Indian thanksgiving fund; all apparently without seriously missing it.

Two further customers conclude the list: H. M. Tennent, on his way to becoming one of the most powerful men in stage circles, and Vernon Castle the American dancer, who both came to Lobb's for their shoes. It was not the coming of Castle which was remembered in the shop but the going. He came in, was fitted with his new shoes, and prepared to leave with them on his feet as they were considerably more comfortable and better fitting than the ones he had had on hitherto. When he reached the door, he was confronted with a London downpour and a muddy pavement. With aplomb, he hailed a passing taxi and as it drew up to the kerb, launched himself in a *grand jête* of Nijinskian proportions to land unscathed on the running board of the taxi, and with a parting wave, disappeared inside the cab with his shoeshine undisturbed.

12

CELEBRITIES AND SLUMPS

WHEN BETSY LOBB and her three young sons returned to their house at Alexandra Road at the end of the War and the bombing, the war-time occupants stayed on. The two in-cumbent families became three and as they were all in some way or another dependent on the fortunes of the business, they had to await increased sales and profits that came with the postwar boom in consumer-spending, before alternative accommodation could be sought.

In these over-crowded but not unhappy circumstances, there was something of a Lobb family co-operative. Meat could be afforded only once a week for the Sunday lunch, and, ironically, some of the cousins had to share a pair of boots turn and turn about. Cousin Fred borrowed a pair to take his girl-friend out for the evening, but as they belonged to the youngest of Betsy Lobb's sons, they were too small and once Fred left the young lady's presence, he was forced to take them off and limp home in his bare feet.

With the upsurge in business, matters improved, the relatives gradually filtered away to alternative accommoda-tion, and Betsy and her sons had the house to themselves again. As the humans left, young Victor and young Eric replaced them with a multitude of pets, from racing pigeons to dogs and parrots; a marsh was created in the garden for frogs caught on fishing-trips to the Hampstead ponds, and by some miracle of parental tolerance a leech was kept in the dining room. The house began to regain some of its former status.

The return to business prosperity makes it quite clear that for all the industrial struggles of the 'twenties, culminating in the General Strike of 1926, an ever increasing number of customers could be found who did not have to resort to strikes to obtain money and who had plenty to spend on luxuries. By 1926, there were over 4,000 customers and the balance sheets were telling a progressively healthier story.

Oddly enough, if the figures are to be believed, the recovery began well before the end of the war. In 1916 sales had picked up to nearly £15,000 and ensured an exceedingly modest net profit of £99, but by 1918 the figures were £16,276 and £2,027 respectively, and by 1920 they had reached an impressive £32,551 and £3,692; William Hunter Lobb's old capital account, now in Betsy Lobb's name, was up to £13,190, reaching a new high of almost £17,000 in 1922. All her sacrifices had paid off.

It was now deemed, in this smiling economic climate, a propitious moment to introduce her second son Victor to the mysteries of bootmaking. Never a keen student at school, Victor was not the most dedicated of bootmakers either. He was good at activities which called for fitness and courage. He was a redoubtable cross-country runner and fencer until he suffered varicose veins at a surprisingly early age. Working at so sedentary an occupation as a bootmaker never fired his imagination, and he spent the next decade flirting with the firm on the days that no more congenial an activity offered itself.

His first flirtation was with agriculture but though he worked on a farm in Gloucestershire, it came to little more than riding to hounds in full hunting regalia and discussing over the stirrup cup agricultural matters of the day. His impact upon the firm was never more than marginal, and that only on the days when there was no horse-show near enough to attend.

His most spectacular break-out from the world of Lobb's was again temporary—a spell in Paris to study singing. This was undertaken with great enthusiasm but eventually came to grief because Victor could not sing in tune, a fact that had been evident to all but Victor before he departed for Paris, but had alas, never been taken into account by himself. When the singing and the bootmaking came to an end, he settled for being a Devonshire farmer, much, one imagines, to the relief of irascible old Tom Moore.

Moore had moved in some other members of his family as Lobb staff, and the firm, with only the occasional appearance of Victor, and the self-effacing William to contradict it, became unofficially known in the trade as Moore's. His autocratic and long regime, from 1916 until 1939, was unchallenged and very rarely even questioned.

The dangers inherent in a business enterprise which in methods and ideas remains completely static in a changing world lay for the moment under the surface. Danger signals were ignored as the rising tide of success seemed to ensure an ever increasing business prosperity. Astonishing as it may seem now, when inflation is unquestioned as an ever present fact of life, the prices of Lobb shoes did not change for the twenty years between the wars. And the firm was, in 1938, exactly as it had been in 1918.

The gay 'twenties and the turbulent 'thirties saw changes but they were in the main confined to the patrons. Old customers died or went elsewhere, but the new additions to the lists of customers were as distinguished as their predecessors.

There are three account books of considerable interest which cover the period up to the outbreak of the Second World War. The first, for 1921-7, has the accounts of 4,132 customers. It not only shows that the firm was retaining the custom of Jonathan Cape, Ronald Firbank, Edward Knoblock, A. E. Matthews, John McCormack, Sir William Orpen, Cole Porter, and Frank Swinnerton among many others, but that an increasing number of famous people were buying their shoes there. Some were coal owners who were buying two and three pairs of shoes at once at a time when they were demanding stringent cuts in miners' wages.

Among the more worthy individuals, were Harold Abrahams, fresh from his gold medal triumph in the 1924 Paris Olympics when his 10.6 seconds dash won him the 100 metres, and Duff Cooper, who resigned as First Lord of the Admiralty when Chamberlain returned from Munich with his useless scrap of paper; Norman Hartnell, later destined to virtually monopolize royal fashion; E. V. Lucas the writer; Compton Mackenzie, who had been a prolific author ever since his first book of poems in 1907 and had served in the Dardanelles in 1915; and the actors Basil Rathbone and Clifton Webb.

Handley Page and Thomas Sopwith, whose aircraft were to make their names world-famous were Lobb customers, too. Sopwith had flown 176 miles in a bi-plane to Belgium as early as 1910, and won a £4,000 prize for the longest ever flight from England in a British machine. During the First World War, Handley Page came into the shop when the few remaining measurement experts were otherwise engaged and, though he never realised it, his feet were measured by an accountant who had never handled a tape in his life! That he remained a customer to the end of his life shows that no harm was done.

Near Page and Sopwith is the name of an Italian senator; now middle-aged, he had seen his inventions change the face of the world, bringing country nearer to country than ever before in history. Guglielmo Marconi's wireless tele- graphy had started with relatively crude equipment sending messages from strangely enough, Penarth to Weston-super- Mare, and had quickly been improved upon. In 1899, he had established communications between France and Eng- land across the channel. By the end of 1902, he and the Governor-General of Canada had stood side by side by a Canadian microphone and sent formal inaugural messages across the Atlantic to the Kings of England and Italy. With- in a few weeks, he had the President of the USA at Cape Cod communicating with the King of England in Cornwall.

Wireless telegraphy was proclaimed a modern miracle, and among the international honours awarded Marconi were the Albert medal, the freedom of Rome, honorary membership of the Royal Society of Arts, and the Nobel Prize for Physics in 1909.

Marconi, at that time living at Marconi House in the Strand, indulged his new leisure with rounds of hunting, cycling, motoring and yachting, all of them naturally in Lobb boots.

The 1928-32 account book gives the broadest of hints that all is not well behind the scenes for the number of customers has fallen by nearly a third to 2,902. The optimist could have been forgiven for overlooking this statistical fact and being bemused by another selection of famous names into thinking that trade was flourishing. But then, blinkered optimists do not make good businessmen.

The 1932-39 accounts show that the decline in the number of customers has been arrested and there is in the 1938 total a very modest increase of 111, bringing the figure up to 3,013. But despite these figures and the fact that Lobb's continued to attract prestigious customers, fewer shoes were being bought. As one would expect in difficult economic times, even the moderately wealthy thought twice before ordering a new pair of boots or shoes, or made do with what they had for a little longer, or when they did buy, bought one pair where in the 'twenties they would have bought two.

Despite the overall decline in the 1928-32 period, Lobb's were catering for new customers from the stage and the flourishing world of the films. By 1932 Lobb's could boast that they were supplying the debonair actor-manager Gerald Du Maurier, famous for his roles as gentlemen crooks such as Raffles or detectives like Bulldog Drummond; and was creator of the twin roles of Mr Darling and Captain Hook in *Peter Pan*. Lobb's also fitted out Adolphe Menjou, accommodating his thin socks and high instep, and Raymond Massey.

From other fields came the multi-talented photographer

and designer Cecil Beaton; one of the most famous names in
bridge, Ely Culbertson, as the card-game ousted billiards
from most upper and upper middle-class houses; and a man
whose advice on business matters would have been valued,
the economist Paul Einzig.

As always there was a good selection of best-selling writers
among the Lobb clients, from Hugh Walpole and Somerset
Maugham (who had small rather delicate feet) to Leslie
Charteris.

Charteris is an interesting man. With his inevitable
monocle and small trim moustache, one wonders to what
extent he had modelled his most famous character Simon
Templar, better known as 'The Saint', on himself. He
started writing when he was seven but claimed that when he
was an undergraduate at Cambridge, he decided to become
a criminal. To perfect his new-chosen craft, he said he read
a great deal of crime fiction, then tried a novel himself to
prove how easy it was. It launched him on a long and
immensely successful career, but it was no overnight success
story and he had had spells as a rubber planter, a seaman,
a bartender and a professional bridge player before his books
reached the best-seller lists. Even then he was quite philo-
sophical and once claimed that his success was 'probably all
quite temporary and in the end I shall be a bum again'.
Needless to say, he never has been, but how valuable an
experience to him as a writer his chequered career must
be.

Another Lobb author, if one may use such a term, was
Michael Arlen, that intriguing chronicler of life in Mayfair.
Although his work, particularly *The Green Hat*, was
accepted as a realistic picture of contemporary manners, it
appears in retrospect as artificial as Firbank's. He once wrote
of himself: 'The writer of the stories of Michael Arlen is an
Armenian born in Bulgaria. On deciding to leave that
wretched country at the age of three, and on arriving at
Dover at the age of four, he asked his way to the nearest
duchess. He was, if one may judge by his stories, mis-

directed. However, he enjoyed, for a short time in the 'twenties, an almost international reputation as a leading authority on matters of no importance whatsoever.'

His own view has a great deal of truth in it.

Less popular than Arlen, but enormously influential in his time, was another customer, James Agate, drama critic of both *The Sunday Times* and the BBC. A bald, florid man, he dressed like a sportsman and on his own admission was never out of debt—indeed, he was once arrested for it. He produced four volumes of autobiography called *Ego 1, 2, 3* and *4* respectively, the title borrowed not from psychological jargon but from his favourite show-harness pony, his hobby being the breeding and exhibiting of such ponies.

The names of such potentates as the Maharajdharja Darbangha (a ledger clerk's nightmare) and the Maharaja of Jaipur recur. Among the English customers was one born in Bombay who would be taking a whole party to India in 1933-4. This was Douglas Robert Jardine, the tall angular cricketer who invariably wore a Harlequin cap and strode on to a cricket field with an assurance that made him perhaps the finest batsman in a crisis the game has ever seen; he was to drive Australian crowds to the point of rioting on the Bodyline tour of 1932-33.

Lobb's also had its lady customers, including a young Sheffield University graduate who won £10,000 from the *Daily Mail* in 1930 by becoming the first woman to fly solo to Australia. This was Amy Johnson, who returned to London to tremendous acclaim, repaid the *Daily Mail* with some round-Britain advertising flights, and spent some of her hard earned prize money on Lobb shoes.

In the 1932-38 accounts, the same mixture prevails. Among the actors were Bela Lugosi (whose sinister features may have given an initial shock to whoever dealt with him in St James's Street) and Wallace Beery. For writers, read Martin de Delincourt and Dennis Wheatley. Representing other art forms, were Paul Czinner the director, Sir Hamilton Harty the conductor, and two distinguished choreographers, George Balanchine and Leonide Massine. Sporting personalities included the trainer, the Hon George Lambton, and the cricketer who played both for England and for India, the Nawab of Pataudi, father of the present cricket-playing Nawab.

Famous customers whose fame sprang mainly from their great wealth were Bernard Docker, Baron Paul Schroeder and Cyril Kleinwort. Two customers, who shall remain anonymous, had their hand-made boots delivered to them—at Pentonville Prison!

There was, moreover, a tall, slightly hunched young man, full of charm, who came to the shop, gave very satisfying references and, being a foreign office diplomat, was naturally welcomed. For the next few years his shoes were made by Lobb's, he paid his bills promptly, and there was never any question that he was other than what he appeared. But then Guy Burgess fooled many people other than Lobb's before he defected to Russia in 1951, the country in whose pay he and his friend Maclean had been for most of their careers. So who paid for Burgess's Lobb boots—the Foreign Office or the Russians?

Lobb boots and shoes (by the 'thirties the shoe had generally replaced the boot as the most common type of footwear) may even have been worn during the momentous political events at the end of the 'thirties, for among the politician customers were Randolph Churchill, Walter Bromley Davenport, and Sir Neville Henderson, the British Ambassador in Berlin, to whom fell the fateful responsibility of delivering Chamberlain's messages to Hitler in the Reichs Chancellery in Berlin.

During the great economic hardships of the 'twenties, a large percentage of the population had given voice to their demand for a share of the unfairly distributed national wealth. Those who were well off gave little attention to strikes and debates about the gold standard, for their standard of living had never been affected by shortages. The middle-classes resented working-class attempts to overtake them, and even a minority Labour government was looked on as a national disaster, but by and large it was still the 'haves' rather than the 'have-nots' who continued to prosper.

When the slumps and depressions of the 'thirties took a firm hold, hardship was no longer restricted to the lower classes. Unemployment was just as unpleasant for white-collar workers as it was for miners. In some ways it was worse, because a boy born in a working-class community in Durham or in the Rhondda Valley was familiar with the situation, whereas one brought up in the pleasant surroundings of a middle-class suburb in Buckinghamshire or Surrey would have lived a life of comparative comfort, and suffered a far greater shock when faced with the loss of income for the first time. Surely the massive turn to the political right in the 'thirties can be explained to some extent as a plea for a government that would restore the standards of living that were quietly but remorselessly slipping away.

Such was the economic situation in which the firm of Lobb's, for all its glittering list of distinguished customers, came to face bankruptcy by the end of the 'thirties. Tom Moore was old; he had no ideas on how to attract more customers or to come to terms with new trends. William Lobb had never asserted any sort of authority over the older man because he was not a forceful leader of men himself. The Royal Warrant had been lost with the death of George V and no-one had had the initiative to attempt to regain it during the short reign of Edward VIII or on the succession of his brother George VI.

With the firm on its last legs, William decided that he must leave to seek work elsewhere. He knew that the firm could no longer provide enough money to support himself and his family, and he understandably though reluctantly gave notice to his mother, still sole proprietor, and to John Lake who still kept the accounts, that he was going. Shortly before he left his younger brother Eric, who had never been associated with the firm before, offered to come into the firm to see if the apparently inevitable could be avoided.

13

BOOTMAKER BY ACCIDENT

THE 1972 VISITOR to Lobb's will not automatically see the present proprietor Eric Lobb. But if he has a special problem, or if he is one of the many regular customers who calls not only to order shoes, but to renew a friendly acquaintanceship, he will be ushered into the small inner sanctum above the main part of the shop. Here he will see a tall, slim but well-built man with grey hair and a beard, his distinguished appearance matched by his ease of manner and an air of unruffled calm.

The firm of Lobb's from 1939 onwards has been built very much in his image and his energy and ideas have carried it from the slough of despond to a flourishing business enterprise—one well versed in the ways of the modern world but retaining an old-world measure of courtesy and tradition of service.

The youngest son of William Hunter Lobb, Eric, was born in 1907 in those prosperous surroundings at St John's Wood. His father died when he was nine so he never knew him well, but in the ordered nursery world of nannies, fathers were anyway rather distant figures. As the youngest child, he was somewhat shy and retiring.

When the catastrophe of his father's death put a temporary end to the family's cosy existence in North London, the quiet child found the infinitely more squalid surroundings of the Brighton basement not to his taste. He followed his brothers to various prep schools, then for a few years at Brighton College, and with the family's return to St John's

Wood, University College School, Hampstead. As often happens to a basically shy child, he did not respond to the challenge of the new surroundings, found school-work irksome, and avoided it where he could. After one piece of slipshod preparation, he was taken aside by a master for the deliverance of the snap verdict that he was 'one of the scum of the earth'. The humiliation of the dismissal worked. He began to apply himself to his books with a new determination that no one would ever be able to say the same about him again.

This was the first sign of the spirit that was to carry him through many another crisis in later life. His new application and industry was applied both to schoolwork and to sport. In schoolwork he reached a competence which preserved him from further humiliation, and he became captain of his house, and of his house's fives, shooting, cricket and rugby teams.

These are all fairly conformist activities. His individuality was better expressed in a more public manner. Partly due to his dexterity on the bugle, he was made the head of the school Officers Training Corps. Part of his duties included sounding the Last Post over silent Hampstead from the roof of the school on Armistice Day.

Although he managed this without any embarrassing fluffed notes or cracks, when it came to the unveiling of a plaque in the school hall as a memorial to the ex-pupils who had been killed in the War, the school's head bugler was passed over, much to his friends' and his own inner chagrin. The ceremony was to be concluded by the Last Post sounded by six buglers from the Brigade of Guards.

With the school hall packed with parents and local dignitaries a bare half-hour before the ceremony was about to start, he was called to the Commanding Officer. It was explained to him that the Guards contingent had failed to arrive and he would have to fill in with another rendering of the Last Post from the roof when he was given a signal from the gallery.

Nervous but full of inner pride that his abilities had been recognised even so late in the day, he repolished his bugle and waited trembling on the roof for a signal from the gallery window. The signal came and he sounded, loudly and faultlessly the Last Post. Flushed with triumph he then rejoined his friends in the hall. Only then was it explained to him that the six Guards had turned up, had lined up on either side of the plaque, had lifted their bugles to within an inch of their lips, and, as the strains of a disembodied Last Post had sounded from some ghostly celestial trumpeter in the sky, had remained frozen in position like half a dozen decorative but mute cherubs. The Guards were not the last people to be pre-empted by the young Lobb who was beginning to find traits inherited from old John Lobb in his make-up.

His secondary education completed, and the business of the firm reaching new heights of prosperity, it was decided that he should not be put to the last like his two brothers before him but given a university education to prepare him for some other career. There were no grants then, but it was found that the family profits could accommodate the expense of sending him to Oxford.

Although he had not passed in Latin, one of the entrance requirements, his college agreed to admit him providing he attended a crammer during the summer before he came, and providing he passed it during his first year.

In his first year, Eric Lobb, who knew no-one, and who had digs well away from the college, worked hard and was one of only two freshmen to get P.Mods. He had the added pleasure of topping the list of passes in Latin. By now, however, doubts had begun to arise concerning his real interest in his chosen subject, French. Particularly when he discovered the existence of the School of Agriculture.

Remembering his childhood interest in pets and his mother's background, and armed with his rather impressive examination results, he was allowed to transfer to study rural economy and agriculture instead of French. It was all so enjoyable and so splendidly removed from the more mundane world of commerce, that he stayed on in Oxford after obtaining his degree in agriculture and did a one year postgraduate diploma in fruit farming.

The one event of 1926 which had such an enormous impact on the life of this country—the General Strike—is very different when looked at through undergraduate eyes. To Eric Lobb and his flannelled friends, it was the biggest opportunity for more undergraduate high spirits they were ever likely to get, and they seized the opportunity with both hands. Where a present-day student would weigh up the issues seriously and, in all probability, take the side of the strikers, the student of the 'twenties was more frivolous. The Oxbridge graduates dug, carried, drove, ferried and loaded for the Government, not, I think, because they were determined to break the strike, but because such tasks, on a temporary basis, looked so attractive. To be whisked away from books and lectures to drive, say, a London Transport bus, was manna from heaven to the bolder spirits in the universities. That nothing would be more abhorrent on a full-time basis is irrelevant.

It was this frivolous spirit which found Eric Lobb and his friends driving in two cars in convoy towards Hull where cargo-laden ships lay idle for the want of dockers, at least according to the public notices in the Oxford Post Office. After a misadventure between the two cars which bent an axle on one of them, Lobb and three others reached Hull at 5 a.m. but were reunited with their fellow-travellers at a hotel in the middle of Hull. They found that the delay on route meant that the Hull docks were now fully manned, and, more to the point, there was an angry Hull crowd outside the hotel thirsting for the blood of black-leg undergraduates.

With that innate British common sense that makes enemies into friends when they come close enough to make human contact (the sort of quality that had miners and strike-breaking soldiers playing football with each other

in Tonypandy, as it did British and German troops in a
Christmas Day ceasefire), the undergraduates mingled with
the crowd and a mass lynching was avoided.

As a result, by the end of the day, Eric Lobb became a
Hull tram-driver, and his companion a conductor. At first,
a policeman on board was obligatory in case an angry band
of strikers was tempted to overturn the vehicle, but after
a few days, the policeman's presence became superfluous as
striker and non-striker alike found it easier to get around
Hull with trams than without. And with the policeman
gone, and the knowledge that it was Cambridge undergraduates who would be responsible for repairing and main-
taining damaged trams, it was time to indulge in a few
tricks like slamming the vehicle into reverse when it reached
top speed. The Oxford undergraduates, always by accident
of course, found ways of damaging trams up to the extent of
£1,000 which kept the Cambridge men up all night.

When the strike ended eventually, the return to work was
heralded by a full-scale university rag throughout the centre
of Hull, and the local population and the imported undergraduates parted on the best of terms.

In 1929, he came down from Oxford, armed with a
degree. His sense of euphoria, induced by the comfort and
high-spirited frivolity of student life in the 'twenties, could
not last long. The real world, as he rapidly found out, was
at that time a grim one: Wall Street had crashed, unemployment was rife, gloom and depression was everywhere and
those not strong enough to swim against a racing tide of
poverty sank.

He had a little capital left in trust for him by his father
but it was insufficient to buy a farm to test all the theories
he had absorbed in his studies. Unfortunately, as he and
others like him struggled for survival, there were a number
of sharks picking off their victims. One of them saw the
Oxford graduate with his now useless degree and diploma,
and moved in for the kill.

This was a gentlemanly property developer who offered

him a partnership in his firm if he would invest in the business. The kindly old gentleman was plausible and patently honest, and so Eric invested his money: it was returned, though without his knowledge, in the form of salary. By the end of the first year, the firm owned several very big white elephants, had pioneered the mews cottage before anyone wanted one, and had no liquid assets at all. The salary stopped when the legacy was exhausted and although Lobb continued to chauffeur the old gentleman around in his car (the other asset that the new partner unwittingly possessed) it all came to an end when the deceits of the past could no longer be concealed. Eric Lobb was again a member of the noble ranks of the unemployed, even larger by 1930 than they had been in 1929.

He was again driven back on his inner resources, and they bolstered him to success in the soul-destroying world of the commercial traveller. He travelled the country selling rubber jointings to factories by the simple expedient of driving into a town and heading for the nearest large chimney. By now, the green Oxford graduate was developing some wisdom in the ways of the world; he exuded enough confidence to persuade factory owners how essential rubber jointings were to their production flow, without ever admitting to them that he had not the slightest idea what rubber jointings were for.

Though sheer force of personality had made him a successful salesman, he found it a tedious way of making a living; he left the firm, but soon had to resort to a succession of selling jobs in order to survive.

Meanwhile, Lobb's firm was declining rapidly, and Betsy Lobb had resorted to taking in paying guests to supplement Eric's none too handsome salary. He joined another property company, protested when the overbearing and incompetent manager sacked a guiltless colleague and was promoted to take the manager's place after he, in turn, was sacked. For the first time since leaving university, he had a respectable, and by 'thirties standards, princely salary of £15 a week.

In his spare time he started a small farming enterprise at the family home at Radlett, Hertfordshire, where the Lobbs had moved, from St John's Wood, in 1925. The four acres, the new farm buildings built by himself, and an assortment of cows, pigs and poultry seemed a wise investment, for even if his job and the family firm came to an end on the same day, the family would not starve. The physical and mental energy required to work long hours as a letting agent, and to double up as a part-time farmer, might have been beyond a lesser man, but Eric Lobb's appetite for work seems to have grown daily more voracious.

It was then that he decided that it would be unjust to allow the family firm that had paid for his happy childhood and his Oxford idyll to go into liquidation without his making an attempt to save it. He wrote to his brother Will and asked if he could join the firm to work without pay. As we now know, William Lobb was already beginning to have grave doubts whether he would be able to stay himself, so he had no objections to the altruistic gesture. In February 1939, Eric Lobb entered the family firm.

Now, unlike every other Lobb over the last seventy years, he had had no training whatever in boot and shoemaking. To make up for this profound ignorance of the trade, he had only youth, enthusiasm, imagination and an unbounded capacity for hard work. None of these qualities were calculated to appeal to old Tom Moore who had held undisputed sway over his tiny St James's Street kingdom since 1916.

It was a piquant situation; the old man who saw the reins of power slipping away from him versus the young man who had had a decade on the receiving end of a tough commercial world and would not allow tradition to prevent him achieving the efficiency necessary for survival. Young Eric Lobb began to turn the firm inside out, while old Tom Moore held out for the methods he had been using fifty years before. There was never open warfare and negotiations between them were always conducted in tones of acid politeness. Nonetheless, everyone on the premises was well aware of the underlying hostility, and the staff, who were mostly elderly, were solidly behind the ageing Tom Moore. With the exception of Tom Moore's younger brother Charlie, of whose slap-dash enthusiasm and genial good humour Tom Moore severely disapproved, the staff viewed the young contender with alarm. Eric Lobb's re-organisation of the firm and its staff included using some of his hard-earned savings for redecorating the premises, and redesigning not only the notepaper but the entire Lobb image. One of the staff looked up from his bench, viewed with disdain the falling plaster and the rising age-old dust and said, just audibly, 'I don't know. I've seen processions, war, Royal funerals and Coronations ... but I've never seen anything like this!' As he shook his head sadly at the follies of youth, he must have epitomised what everyone felt.

The staff had barely begun to grasp what was happening around them, when in September 1939 a much larger menace to the welfare of both men and management loomed —the outbreak of war.

The autocratic Frederick
Richards, brother-in-law
of the founder

Tom Moore, a manager in the
Richards tradition, casts a stern
: over Ernest Sandford's accounts.
The portrait on the wall above is
of old John Lobb

Tom Moore's younger brother
Charlie demonstrates the
noble art of clicking

A section of the Lobb
library of lasts

Lobb's today, at 9 St James's Street

14

LEST WE FORGET

WITH BROTHER William now installed in the Ministry of Information where his knowledge of French got him a place, Eric Lobb was fighting a battle on two fronts. Just before the fall of France John Lake, the firm's accountant for many years, pointed out to Betsy and Eric Lobb that there was no money to pay the men the following week. After a moment's hesitation in totting up what little of his savings remained, Eric said he would write a cheque to cover the amount. John Lake looked dubious, reminded them that the Channel ports could fall by the end of the week and that their Paris business would then be in German hands.

Still full of enthusiasm for defying fate where possible, Eric insisted on putting his good money after the bad. For his pains, the Channel ports fell six days later.

On the occupation of Paris, the Paris shop duly fell into German hands although the staff hid the lasts beforehand. Financial credit was arbitrarily transferred to Berlin, the shop looted, and the unfortunate English manager Mr Hope-Boyce interned at the camp in Saint-Denis. For all anyone knew, London might follow before the end of the conflict—most of the world thought it likely.

In common with so many of the British male population, Eric Lobb decided that he had no business in concerning himself with the problems of a small ailing family firm when the very safety of the country was in peril. He decided to go to fight in the war. At his age, he was naturally a volunteer, but the choice of service was not easy. Influenced by a friend on whose boat Eric had had his very limited sailing experience, the prospective admiral applied, with his friend, to the Navy for admission under the yachtsman's entry scheme. They were called for interview.

The night before the interview, Eric Lobb became aware that he would have to answer some technical questions on navigation and kindred subjects, and armed with his friend's sailing manual he tried some last-minute swotting. With only the first chapter on the kinds and functions of buoys digested, the applicant fell asleep. Next morning, as it happened, three high-ranking naval officers interviewed him, and for quarter of an hour were held spell-bound by the candidate's comprehensive and instant answers on buoys. They then put a chart on the table with two model ships on it, informed Lobb that he was captain of one of them, and proceeded to push the models at a steady rate of knots on a collision course. 'Now, Mr Lobb,' one of them asked, 'what would you do in this situation?' Silence reigned.

Unable or unwilling to conclude that a man who knew so much about buoys could be totally ignorant of every other nautical practice, the officer slowed the models down to a crawl and said, 'Come, come, Mr Lobb, you remember the old verse ...'

'Oh, yes, the old verse. Yes. Yes. It's just slipped my mind for a moment.'

Longer silence.

'Come on, come on. If to starboard red appear ...'

'Oh yes, yes. Of course. If to starboard red appear, um, um, ah, um. If to starboard red appear. Tumti-tum-ti-uh ... steer clear?'

'Exactly, Mr Lobb. Yes, I'm sure we'll be able to find you something.'

This grand and novel entrance to the Navy was only prevented by a medical examination which revealed that Eric Lobb was colour-blind, and was therefore unable to distinguish between red and green, an inability the navy regretfully regarded as too much of a hazard; the naval career ended there and then.

An application to join the Middlesex Regiment failed by a few days, which was just as well for the future of Lobb's, and for Eric Lobb himself, considering the heavy casualties the regiment suffered at Calais. That left the Air Force. This time, the candidate was honest enough to reveal his colour-blindness at the outset. In some capacities that did not matter and Rear-Gunner E. Lobb was told to report to Torquay the following week to commence duties. This set in motion a chain of coincidences of the kind that seem inseparable from the story of Lobb's, and shows how desperately near closure they have been.

In the few days before Eric Lobb was due to report, Tom Moore decided to quit. The twin assaults of the young upstart and the increase in German bombing raids had taken their toll. He decided Lobb's of London was no place to see out a prolonged and dangerous war and he gave, after fifty-seven years service, one week's notice that he was leaving.

So, instead of being able to leave the firm for the Air Force, knowing that an experienced if reactionary manager would be in charge, Eric Lobb was forced to admit that this was indeed the end, at least until the end of the war, of a family firm just approaching its seventy-fifth birthday. On application, he was given an extra week to liquidate the firm before he reported.

The very next day, there was another communication in the post to change everything. It was considered necessary to the prestige of Britain and British industry for the world-famous firm of Lobb's to continue and to show the world that whatever the Germans did about it London's West End was carrying on. Rear-Gunner Lobb's call-up was meanwhile suspended indefinitely.

For the next five years, through blitz, shortage and the attendant war-time problem of form-filling by the ream, Eric Lobb and his firm carried on making high-class footwear and supplying people all over the world. By using the library of lasts and sending out self-measurement instructions and forms, Lobb's built up orders from America— North and South, Mexico, South Africa, Australia, Canada, India, Newfoundland, Palestine, Egypt, Switzerland, Spain, Portugal and France and, even in 1940, Italy and Japan; and Lobb boots and shoes were worn in every theatre of war.

*

In the Yale University Department of History, in New Haven, Connecticut, a Faculty Committee on War Literature was set up under the chairmanship of Sherman Kent to collect material on the European War. Amongst its papers, posters and ephemera of war is the following letter which gives a full picture of the hazards and discomforts of life at Lobb's in 1941:

Dr. Sherman Kent,   7th January, 1941
Yale Station,
New Haven,
Conn., U.S.A.

Dear Sir,
    Mr W. S. Lewis of Farmington, Connecticut, has asked me to send you some details of work in London, under the present war-time conditions.
    Up to August 1940 the chief visible signs of the war were the many uniforms of all kinds to be seen in the streets, the reduction of traffic by about one half—mainly due to petrol rationing—and the material precautions taken against invasion and the effects of bombing.
    The enclosed photograph of my own premises will give you an idea of the appearance of many of the shop windows in London before the bombing began: now, alas! the glass, although it was hoped to protect it somewhat by strips of paper and other means, has in most cases disappeared and of my own six plate glass windows two only remain intact, the others having been blasted out by two separate bombings.
    Every building where work proceeds during the raids has some form of shelter and my own, which is typical of many, has the entrance to its basement screened by sandbags: this gives protection against blast and splinters from near-by bombs but, in all but the

strongest and deepest shelters, a direct hit would of course be fatal.

Although it was not until 29th. August that Central London was first bombed it was only a fortnight earlier that nearly 500 German aeroplanes were brought down over Britain within one week. By the middle of September air-raid warnings and 'all clears' were literally sounding on the sirens all day and all night and it did not take long for 'familiarity to breed contempt'. This was particularly so in the case of the day raider as, owing to the complete mastery by the R.A.F. the Londoner knew that only an occasional raider could get through and that then its chances of escape were small; when this happened people would gather in the streets and watch the 'dog fights' between the R.A.F. and the raider—or rather, they would watch the trails of smoke, like skywriting, left by the machines which were themselves too high to be visible.

On 10th September I was walking along Jermyn Street towards St James's Street when a warning was sounded and, shortly after a low flying aeroplane was heard followed by some loud bangs; people in the street who, until then had taken little notice of the warning, quickly took cover and I stepped into a hotel for shelter. I mention this incident because it was the occasion when Buckingham Palace was bombed for the first time.

When the day raids were at their height it was the custom in my firm to go to the basement, not when the sirens first sounded, but only if guns or bombs were heard. Subsequently even these noises became so familiar that now work proceeds as in normal times; this may sound like bravado but when it is realised that many of the explosions are from time bombs in areas that have been cleared by the police and that, to-day, we often hear the dynamiting of the ruined City buildings, you will understand how the first fear which we undoubtedly experienced has been replaced by our present indifference.

Strangely enough, as I write to-day, we have had our first day-time warnings for many weeks but the novelty has quite worn off and the sirens were hardly commented on, the only emotion that the gunfire seemed to arouse being one of annoyance at the slight interruption to the day's work.

You will be wondering at the results of the bombing; as far as the West End is concerned I know of very few firms that have gone out of business as a result of being hit. I have, on the other hand, seen the most total and hideous wreckage of very old establishments and, almost before the dust and smoke has died down, a notice has appeared on the debris giving the address of the firm's new premises.

Where only broken glass or minor damage has occurred a spirited notice such as 'Bloody but unbowed' will be seen or, in a more humorous vein, 'This is nothing, you should see our branch in Berlin!' or 'We are more open than usual' and again, 'We are blasted well open!'

Needless to say, most firms have duplicate records in country offices and, in my own case, apart from duplicating all material of importance, I have had the wooden 'lasts', which represent the feet of all my customers and on which all their boots and shoes are made, taken outside London; individual pairs are brought up as orders are received and returned to the country when the work has been carried out. This has proved to be a wise precaution as our lasts store, which is separate from our shop premises, has since been bombed to the ground.

As to my staff, all the young men are in the Services and those left are working harder and doing other jobs besides their normal ones. The 'black-out' has reduced our working day by one hour as we close at 5 p.m. instead of 6 and many firms close as early as 4 p.m. To make up for this it is necessary to work on a Saturday afternoon, when normally we should be closed, and this is done without demur.

Time bombs have caused the temporary removal from their homes of several of my men but I am thankful to say that only one has so far had to abandon his house and this was without injury to himself or his family.

The Germans, as you know, are suggesting that their bombing has resulted in the dislocation of all work in London. In my own small sphere I can only say that we have not yet had to turn down a single order although the volume of our business was greater in 1940 than in 1939. Orders for the fighting services are continually being carried out at short notice and, in every week of the war so far, we have sent shipments abroad which, with one exception, have been delivered safely; the exception referred to was in the case of two pairs of shoes which were returned damaged—they had not been lost.

Since the fall of France I have collected one copy only of every foreign stamp that comes to us in the course of business: at present I have some 60 different stamps covering 20 countries or states but this is, of course, no real indication of the extent of our foreign trade as I have kept no duplicates.

Most of our leather is imported and, with the exception of patent —which used to come from Germany—we have experienced no shortage so far. Owing to the fact that evening shoes are not now required in England we have only needed a small quantity of patent leather for export and this has been easily obtainable. Apart from leathers we also require linen, silk, satin, velvet, and metal goods

such as spurs, etc. and all of these we are still able to obtain
without difficulty.

I do not pretend that London life has not altered—it has to an
unbelievable degree—but I give the above examples to show that,
in my experience, work is able to proceed without much interruption.

We work harder and with fewer men; we have all manner of
inconveniences; 'diversion' notices appear overnight on roads made
unusable by bombs; transport from home to work is sometimes
difficult and overcrowded; sleep is interrupted; pleasures are few and
far between.

In spite of these and many more difficulties, however, it is true
to say that, so fixed is the purpose of the average Londoner to
carry on through it all, that these results of the war are taken for
granted and he cares for nothing but the playing of his part towards
its successful conclusion.

I hope that I may have added a little to your knowledge of the
West End of London as affected by the war; the subject, as you
will realise, is a large one with which to deal in the space of a letter
and I write only as a business man who has spent every working
day throughout the whole period of the war so far in London. I
look forward to doing the same for the rest of the war and, in this,
I share the hope and expectation of millions of others whose work
lies there.

In conclusion, may I say that I and many others have derived
great encouragement from the enthusiastic letters which are continually arriving from our customers in the U.S.A.

> I am, Sir,
> Yours faithfully,
> Eric Lobb

Such was the spirit that carried the ordinary Londoner
through the War—not the hero, whose exploits are known
to all, but the common man in the street.

Just as remarkable was Eric Lobb's phenomenal energy.
Bit by bit, he took home to Radlett all the order books and
ledgers, and, even more important, the precious and irre-
placeable lasts. These lasts were taken back and forth for
the duration of the war by the sackful, for one bomb could
have destroyed them all and suspended the firm's activities
for good. On Sundays they had to be sorted and the correct
ones found for Monday morning's work. It was on the day

after the final sackful had been taken to Radlett that the last store was blown to smithereens by a direct hit.

Also at Radlett, he typed all the firm's correspondence, during the spare time he did not have, for he was running the four-acre farm at the same time, and the correspondence for that had to be written by hand on the train to town in the mornings. Although the shop was closed early by law, he stayed until after 6 p.m. to cope with the bookkeeping. This routine was followed for the next five years, except when Eric was carrying out Home Guard duties, at which times he slept in a garage. The Radlett farming enterprise was so successful as an economic unit that it was featured in the *Illustrated Sporting and Dramatic News* of October 1940 as an example of the necessary intensive use of land.

The Lobb premises were bombed six times, and the task of picking up broken glass and assorted boots, shrapnel and plaster became a morning ritual. Staff morale was difficult to maintain for it was no pleasant thing to work while bombs initially and later the even more dreadful rockets, fell around them. On one of these occasions, Jim Saunders was dealing with a distinguished Admiral when the characteristic noise of a V.I got alarmingly close, followed by the inevitable and menacing silence before the explosion on impact. Jim, prevented by social convention from joining the scramble to the basement, gripped the nearest table and held on grimly. The Admiral gripped the other end and they stood silent and static, neither acknowledging that there was anything unusual about their postures, until the bang a few streets away showed that danger was over.

In these fraught circumstances Charlie Moore could usually be counted upon for some comic relief. When another Admiral came in fuming about some mistake which had been made in his order, Charlie was unperturbed. He took some time to calm the Admiral down and to absorb the broadsides being loosed off at him. When the pacified gentleman eventually came to leave, Charlie had, as usual the last word. He called the Admiral back into the shop, dusted him down with a clothes brush and said,

'That's better, sir. We don't mind you coming into the shop with dandruff on your collar, but we can't have you leaving like it.'

This amiable and well-liked man died in 1963; he, above all others, had been responsible for feeding Eric Lobb with the technical background Eric, unlike his forbears, lacked. That was one reason why Eric Lobb went down to Fulham to find Charlie one morning when he had failed to turn up at Lobb's after a night of heavy bombing. When he got there there was not much of a street left, but in a front garden before a smoking pile of rubble stood Charlie and his wife. In fact, he had glass splinters in both eyes and had to be taken to hospital, but his only reaction when he saw his employer was to say, 'Morning, guvnor. Bit of trouble in the night but I'll be in a bit later.'

After a short spell in hospital where his sight was saved, he was back at Lobb's and delighting and infuriating his colleagues by turn. The same went for one peer of the realm who was very deaf and used an ear trumpet. Charlie was equally deaf and after spending some time talking at cross purposes, his Lordship realised the fact, with the result that the two completed their business shouting at one another and passing an ear trumpet back and fore like a baton.

The premises at 55 St James's Street started by old John Lobb were destroyed in 1944 when two bombs dropped just behind them, lifted the whole structure into the air, and settled it down again with a crack all round the foundations. Because of the danger of the whole edifice collapsing around their ears, Lobb's were forced to move into a new building; luckily enough they found one at 26 St James's Street, although the water flooding the basement, and the plaster, glass and tin-hats littering the floor made it look a worse proposition than number 55. (Nine years later, in 1955, when the old mahogany façade of number 55 was due for demolition, Eric Lobb intervened and was able to buy it from the contractor for its sentimental and historic value for £12 10s!; he transported it out to Radlett where it still does service as a summer house.)

Lobb's saw out the rest of the war at number 26 and Eric Lobb always ensured his men got a holiday, though he never managed to take one himself. Despite bomb damage they were only looted once, and then only on a very minor scale. One night at 1 a.m., Eric Lobb received a telephone call from his taxi-driver cousin who had been driving up St James's Street and, hearing a flying bomb close at hand, had vacated his cab and lain in the gutter.

'... And then,' he went on, 'I heard the bang and all the windows of your shop were blown in.'

'Oh, yes?' (By now this was a common occurrence.)

'Yes. There was a policeman there.'

'Oh yes, what did he do?'

'Snatched a pair of boots from your window and ran like hell!'

There were also, unfortunately, the tragedies that brought home the desperate nature of the struggle in which the nation was involved. One customer, and a faithful one, was Admiral Sir Tom Phillips who with six hundred others drowned when the *Prince of Wales* and the *Repulse* were sunk by the Japanese in December 1942. Another was General Sikorski, lost on a flight in 1943, a disaster which was to receive fresh attention in 1967 with Rolf Hochhuth's play *Soldiers* speculating on the supposed involvement of Winston Churchill in the accident.

As well as the deaths of the famous, there were two incidents involving less distinguished Lobb customers which give an added poignancy to a glance through the war-time records.

In June 1942, a Willie Radcliffe of the 3rd Parachute Battalion wrote to Lobb's about his boots, and added a post-script which said—'Without wishing to pay flowery compliments, may I say that I have always looked upon your London shoes as representing everything that is best in

English workmanship.' Just eleven months later, his friend
Robert Wace wrote:

Dear Mr Lobb,
I have sad, sad news. Willo Radcliffe has been killed in action.
I know he would have liked you to hear this personally.
He was a fine Englishman—dead game.
I only met you through him and I well remember his saying; 'If I
"go", Bill, see that Gilbert and Edward go to Lobb's. That means a
lot.'
I am the guardian of the twins—his sons.
You must look after them as you did him.
While you and I may be feeling sad, he would say, 'Now we go into
attack'.
There was a man.

> Yours sincerely,
> Robert Wace.

Such words made the struggle of continuing seem that much
more worthwhile, as did the young commando who came in
in the early part of the war asking for a pair of boots that
would be completely silent. He returned after the War
without them and was wearing a cheap, clumsy pair which
he took off and placed on the counter once he had been
fitted. He then admitted that the cheap boots had been made
for him by Polish prisoners of war in a concentration camp
in Germany. His Lobb boots had been taken from him when
he got there. Worse, when the War began to go against the
Germans, the guards went through the camp shooting any
English officers they could find. He had successfully hidden
and survived; his best friend had been found and shot.

In case it seems unreasonable to revive such memories
three decades on, it is worth recalling the advice of the
famous American customer who came to Lobb's when card-
board filled the windows and plaster was falling from the
walls. This was Edward G. Robinson. He looked around
and said, in those famous gravelly tones, 'You been bombed,
Mr Lobb?'

'Yes, quite a few times but we're trying to forget it.'

'No! You must NEVER forget.'

15

AMERICAN HOSPITALITY

FROM THE tail end of the 'thirties, when Eric Lobb first entered the firm, throughout the 'forties that drab, queue-ridden age of rationing and shortage, there were problems to face and policies to inaugurate.

His aims were to enhance the prestige of the firm so that it should be worthy of its own past, and to make it once more a viable economic proposition. His boundless energy stood him in good stead for he refused to sit in the shop waiting for orders, but went out looking for them himself. He made provincial tours in Britain making himself available for consultations and measuring sessions, and sent out circulars to remind old customers of the firm's continued existence and explain the Lobb services to the uninitiated. These activities were dovetailed with his calls as a one-man debt-collector when, after a reasonable interval, the badly-needed cash failed to materialise after orders had been completed and delivered.

What none of the new customers who met him on his first tour in 1940 realised, was that the latest bootmaking Lobb was hardly steeped in the mystique of the hand-sewn craft, with a lifetime's experience behind him, but had learned to measure feet in a ten-minute session with his mother and brother a few days before the tour had started! Fortunately, he made no errors and many of the 'guinea-pigs' remained life-long customers.

He joined the Master Bootmakers' Association so that the firm and the industry could speak with a united voice on their war and postwar problems. (He is now the body's president). Eric's father, William Hunter Lobb, had been a member of the Association until 1914, when he had resigned because some of the members failed to uphold its policy in a strike; Lobb's had remained outside ever since.

He also proceeded to work for another revival of past procedure, for the firm to again become holders of a Royal Warrant. The appointment had ceased with the death of Edward VII, and due to lack of imagination and initiative within the firm had been long forgotten. He was so successful that by 1963, when a Warrant as Royal Bootmaker had been awarded by Her Majesty the Queen to add to the one held from His Royal Highness the Duke of Edinburgh since 1956, Lobb's were one of the few firms who could claim to supply both the Royal couple together with other members of the Royal Family; they continue to do so to this day.

The 'forties were an uphill struggle. To prosper in a country trying desperately to settle the accumulated debts and losses of a long arduous war far beyond its normal resources was no easy matter, and such crises as the fuel shortage of 1947 added to the difficulties. (The Minister of Fuel and Power, Emmanuel Shinwell, was irreverently known at Lobb's as the 'Minister of Foul and Pure' at this time.)

Apart from the black-marketeers, the spivs and the fiddlers, there were several who tried, unsuccessfully, to obtain Lobb shoes without the requisite nine coupons, only to be firmly shown the door. There was only one place where there was enough money in circulation to line the pockets of potential Lobb customers. This was, of course, America, and by 1949 the intrepid Eric Lobb had embarked on the *Queen Mary* to follow up a circular letter offering his services. The fare and the expenses were paid from a bank overdraft, and the bank manager insisted on retaining the deeds of the family house at Radlett as security for the loan.

Two days before he embarked, the telephone rang in his

office. The call came from America, from an old Lobb customer, Mr Benjamin Kulp, a man he had never met. Kulp offered his hospitality to the English bootmaker, urging him to indulge himself in a two-week stay on the Kulp ranch in Arkansas. Eric Lobb politely explained that the itinerary for his stay was fully booked and would not permit a two-week holiday in the middle. He forbore to add that he would have to work flat out for the whole duration if he were to repay the costs of the trip.

Kulp, with that genial but irresistible firmness that characterises Americans, insisted, and before the refusal could be repeated had rung off, with the parting shot that his man would be meeting Lobb in New York. For once defeated, Eric Lobb hurriedly re-arranged his itinerary.

When he reached New York, the hotel, the food and the general atmosphere of affluence seemed to a war-worn Englishman like the land of milk and honey must have seemed to the followers of Moses. While on the boat, he had received a cable from Kulp telling him to be on the look-out for a man wearing a red and green tie, who would be waiting for him. In theory this was a good system of identification, but of course red and green were exactly the two colours which Eric Lobb was totally incapable of recognising. Fortunately, by searching through the passengers' luggage stacked in alphabetical order, the Kulp chauffeur found him instead, and escorted him to his New York hotel.

Before he had had time to readjust to the sounds and bustle of this noisy, dangerous and exciting city, he had the first indication that transatlantic business affairs might not be conducted with the genteel reserve that typified the relationship of an English gentleman and his bootmaker. As he stood in the lobby with his luggage around him (naïvely unaware that a tip had to be forthcoming *before* anyone was likely to move it) a full-blown Admiral of the US Fleet strode through to be greeted by the bell-boy with a 'Hiya, Admiral!' Clearly, he was in a very different country.

If he had not believed it then, he would have believed it a few weeks later when he received a call at his Boston hotel from a customer to come out to his home and to measure him up for a pair of Lobb shoes as a memento of a day made memorable by the purchase of a large bank. The ubiquitous Kulp driver (one appeared as if by magic on every part of the tour) was told to call later in the afternoon, not to the hotel, but to the man's home to collect Eric Lobb.

When Lobb got to the house just outside Boston, a wild party was in progress with mine host even further in his cups than the guests. The royal bootmaker was plied with whisky and told to measure every guest, relative and servant in the house for Lobb shoes as presents from the new bank-owner. All, that is, except the butler, of whom the host said, 'Not him, I'm firing the bastard anyway.'

The measuring session completed, Lobb was asked to wait for the host's son who had to be given Lobb shoes too. Meanwhile, the Kulp chauffeur arrived at the house. The driver was duly brought in. The host, who was obviously hazy on appearances by now, fell on his neck and exclaimed, 'You're back, my son, I want you to be measured for a pair of Bobb loots!' The bootmaker and his driver left quietly—they never saw the son, although persumably when he did turn up, he was mistaken in turn for someone else.

Armed with an order like the bank-buyer's, and others equally profitable if less bizarre, Eric Lobb was now ready for his stay on the Kulp ranch. He flew in to Little Rock airport with the realisation dawning that he had not the slightest idea what Kulp looked like. In the crowded and unfamiliar airport lounge, inspiration dawned. He walked around discreetly eyeing the footwear until recognising a pair of Lobb shoes—their owner, fortunately, was Benjamin Kulp.

For the next two weeks, the hospitality was on the grand scale. Eric Lobb was supplied with a Buick and a horse for any travelling or recreation he wished. Because he gave voice to his admiration of the peasant bedspreads in his room, a pair was sent off to his ship ready to be taken back with him to England. There were parties of Kulp friends invited every night to the ranch and duly invited or bullied into ordering Lobb shoes. As a grand finale to the two weeks, Eric Lobb was given a pair of jeans, a T-shirt and a peaked cap (not unnaturally, this was the first time in his life he had ever worn such an outfit) and taken off by Kulp to his cabin in the mountains. Such garb, Kulp explained, was necessary if anyone was to speak to them in the local bars.

On the way back from the mountains, in the company of this delightful and witty man, Eric Lobb plucked up enough courage to ask what was, more than ever, the sixty-four million dollar question.

'Mr Kulp, you have been the finest host a man could wish for, you've treated me with the kind of hospitality that's normally given royalty. And all this to a man you've never met before. I must ask you. Why?'

Benjamin Kulp paused and smiled saying, 'Well, I just kinda liked your letters ...!'

When Lobb returned to London he had the satisfaction of knowing that the gamble had paid off, for he brought back orders which more than paid the expenses of the trip, and he came back with treasured memories of the new friends like Benjamin Kulp he had made in the States.

It was with very different feelings however that he came back from his second trip in 1951. This was a return visit to follow up the success of the last one when he had started out with a list of 600 names and little else besides. This time he was lucky to come back alive.

One stop on his 1951 itinerary was Washington, where he made the acquaintance of Justice William O. Douglas of the Supreme Court. The Supreme Court Justice was measured for a pair of boots, and as Eric Lobb had read of the terrible horse-riding accident that had befallen Douglas in which he broke twenty-three ribs, he complimented Douglas on his recovery. The judge told him how lucky he was to be alive thanks to the medical attention he had received.

The story had a great deal more than surface meaning within a few weeks.

In company with his American wife, who was some five months pregnant, Eric flew to Arizona for a holiday with friends before continuing his whistle-stop tour of the country. The couple were in a car with two other people when they were rammed by another car travelling at high speed. In this accident, the other two occupants of the car were killed, his wife and her unborn child by some miracle were relatively unharmed physically, and he himself was rushed to an Arizona hospital in a critical condition.

As he lay there mostly unconscious for five days, it emerged that he had fractured his skull and broken eighteen ribs, amongst other injuries; the staff of the hospital thought that he had no chance of living.

They did not know the inherited Lobb spirit or of his own tremendous capacity for absorbing punishment and coming back for more. His first question on temporarily regaining consciousness was, 'Am I going to die?.' The doctor at the bedside lied and said it was out of the question.

'You'd better tell me because I've a few things to tidy up first if I am' was the calm rejoinder before he slipped back into oblivion. Recover he did, against expectation, and after his stay in hospital he caught the same ship back to England he had been booked on before the accident. After a six month convalescence at Radlett, and one false attempt, he started back to Lobb's, having rid himself of the handicap of blacking out whenever he changed his position from vertical to horizontal or *vice versa*. A New York specialist told him that it would take twenty years to recover from all the side-effects, a prediction which proved broadly accurate, though he now plays tennis, sails and takes physical exercise as if none of it had happened.

There was a welcome sequel to the trip—a letter from Justice Douglas who had heard of Eric Lobb's accident and wrote to award him the honorary vice-presidency of the newly formed Broken Ribs Society, the President of which was himself with the slightly superior claim of twenty-three ribs against Eric's eighteen. Eric was graciously pleased to accept the offer and to defer to the American's claim for the top office. And if Eric Lobb made it back to the tennis court after such damage, Justice Douglas was not going to let a small accident slow him down either. In 1954, he and thirty-six others hiked about 180 miles from Maryland to Washington D.C. Only nine of the thirty-seven finished the course and most fell out with foot trouble. But not Justice Douglas, a fighter in the Lobb tradition. He wrote later, 'The walking boots you made for me in 1953 are the best I have ever had. I wore them on the 180-mile hike from Cumberland, Maryland to Washington, D.C. in March 1954. They carried me through all sorts of terrain without trouble of any kind. I had no blisters or abrasions of any kind during those eight days. My feet were in excellent condition every night. I wish you would pass on to your bootmakers my appreciation for their fine work.'

During Eric Lobb's prolonged absence from the firm while he convalesced, his brother William was in command. William had rejoined the firm at the end of the War, after leaving his war-time post at the Ministry of Information; he had applied for a job by letter to the brother who six years earlier had applied to him to work for nothing! Naturally, Eric Lobb was delighted to have so expert a craftsman and pleasant a colleague in harness with him, and they became equal partners in 1950 with Betsy Lobb, for so long sole proprietor. The triumvirate only dissolved when Betsy Lobb died in 1956, and though the two brothers continued together thereafter, Eric was left as the sole proprietor when his brother William died in 1963. (To ensure that there will still be a Lobb at Lobb's in the future John Hunter Lobb, William's son, is working at St James's Street today; he undertook a trip to America for the firm in 1966. And, unlike his uncle he has had a thorough grounding in clicking, closing *et al.*)

Gradually the trials and tribulations of the 'forties gave

way to the more prosperous 'fifties, when the firm progressed steadily and began to take over other firms—fourteen, so far—a process which was always a wrench on funds, and which brought many organisational problems. Several of these firms had formerly been rivals, but found themselves unequal to the problems of perpetuating an old-fashioned bootmaking business in a modern world. Without the flair and the salesmanship of Eric Lobb, Lobb's might have suffered the same fate.

With the 'sixties the firm continued to expand, and it remains a flourishing business. Their prices over the years give a remarkable indication of the speed of post-war inflation. The pair of shoes which Lord Alfred Douglas bought in 1902, by 1942 would have cost him about £6 12s 6d, an increase of 300 per cent in forty years, which is about what one would expect. But from then on, prices have had to increase thick and fast as costs of materials and labour have spiralled. In 1947, Bosie would have had to pay £12 18s 9d; in 1953 £17 6s 3d; in 1958 £21; in 1961 £23 2s 0d, and by 1972 well over £50 to get approximately the same sort of shoe and service he got fifty years before.

Price trends are not always so depressing. *Punch*, referring to a *Sunday Times* 'Atticus' item about Lobb's commented in 1956: 'Readers of a Sunday causerie felt cheated recently when they were told about a Mayfair shop whose ostrich-leather shoes at thirty-five guineas are "so much in demand that many clients find it cheaper to bring their own skins". The price for shoes in this material wasn't quoted.'

And as prices changed, so did premises again. To make room for the construction of the *Economist* tower block, the firm was forced in 1962 to move down the road to their present address at Byron House, 7-9 St James's Street, where they will remain, unless some other unforeseen circumstance uproots them yet again. So far they have been happier there than their distinguished predecessor Lord Byron, who lived for a while in the 'Residential Quarters for Noblemen and Gentlemen of High Rank' on the site at number 8. After he had been there a very short while, he was laid up with a stone in the kidney, his finances were in an unholy mess; Lady Caroline Lamb is supposed to have invaded his privacy there dressed as a page and outstayed her welcome. Unlike Byron, Lobb's have found the spot an eminently friendly environment.

16

PLUS ÇA CHANGE ...

WHEN JEAN-BAPTISTE ALPHONSE KARR, the French novelist, wrote *Plus Ça Change, plus c'est la Meme Chose*, he could almost have been thinking of his contemporary, old John Lobb, setting out on the adventures that eventually led to the existence of the world's greatest bootmakers in present-day St James's Street. Several generations of families have been employed there. Workman has been succeeded by son, grandson and great-grandson. Prices have soared to a level John Lobb would have thought impossible. Famous customers have died, and been replaced by celebrities of succeeding eras. And yet, for all that, the firm has changed very little in its basic principles: it remains a sanctuary from the cheap and the shoddy, where employees and customers alike take an interest in the craft of hand-sewn boots and shoes.

One of the Lobb workmen recently wrote down the following song:

> I live and I work, in a cellar below,
> Where I sit and I sing at my ease.
> I work not at bench or a vice if you please,
> The work is all done on my knees.
>
> With my hammer and pinchers,
> My heel ball and wax,
> My bristles and flax,
> My lapstone and tacks,
> I cobble old boots and I stitch up the cracks—
> Just a jolly old cobbler am I.

Like my pal the tailor, my cabbage* I sell,
That's when I return to the last.
But when I'm stony broke and I can't get the boot,
That's when I return to the last.

With my hammer and pinchers,
My heel ball and wax, etc.

Though the age of the song is unknown, and it is unlikely to have been written down before, one can imagine how easily it might have come from the mouths of one of the characters in *The Shoemaker's Holiday*, the play mentioned earlier, written in 1599. To look at Lobb's is to look at history.

Few customers come only to look at history when they come to Lobb's. What brings them in is the knowledge that they will be supplied with footwear in accordance with their wealth or social status. Account books since 1945 read like editions of the *International Who's Who*. Today's Lobb customer can know that he is putting his foot into a personally tailored replica of shoes and boots made for and worn by monarchs such as King Hussein of Jordan, authors like Peter Cheyney, John Paddy Carstairs, and Roald Dahl, Prime Ministers such as Harold Macmillan, Chancellors of the Exchequer such as Anthony Barber, designers such as Hardy Amies, peers such as the Duke of Bedford, magnates such as Charles Clore, cricketers such as Denis Compton and Godfrey Evans, actors such as Cyril Cusack and Jack Buchanan, impresarios such as Jack Hylton, singers such as Donovan, and film stars such as Orson Welles, Frank Sinatra, Gregory Peck, Peter O'Toole, Laurence Harvey and Katherine Hepburn, to name but a very random selection.

If he or she is lucky enough, the customer may leave the shop having witnessed some curious occurrence on the august premises.

---

* Cabbage: the remnants and off-cuts of the hide or the cloth which are scrapped or sold after the necessary patterns have been cut out.

They may meet the White Russian who, after concluding his business with Lobb's, turns at the doorway to fling all his loose change in behind him for the staff to scrabble for on the carpet; or the American who comes over to Britain about once a year, sticks his head around the door and says, 'Make me as many boots as you can by the end of the month before I go back'. (Another customer is more discreet: his secretary rings up and asks for boots and shoes to be made to his last—a thousand pounds' worth at a time.) Another customer's standing order is, 'Twelve assorted pairs. I'll leave the rest to you!'

Three visits have been very nostalgic occasions for the present proprietor. The first was from the one-time Oxford Blue and rugby captain, Tommy Gubb. Gubb, a South African, was at Oxford with Eric Lobb, though Eric was only a humble college footballer, of far lower status than the Blue who, even more than the Oxford captains of today, was treated like a god among men. They never exchanged conversation, but after a particularly well-lubricated rugby supper for the college teams, Eric Lobb lurched from his college entrance to see a large gentleman urinating against the back-wheel of his (Eric's) motor-car. Just as he was about to remonstrate with the vandal, he realised that it was Gubb, thought better of it, and drove quietly away.

Some thirty years later a South African came to the shop. As the order form made clear, it was T. Gubb Esq. on a visit to England. When he realised who it was, Eric Lobb approached him.

'Mr Gubb?'

'Yes, that's right.'

'The Tommy Gubb who captained Oxford in the 'twenties?'

'Yes, yes! You remember that? That's marvellous. That's made my whole trip to England, that someone should remember that.'

'Well, actually, what I really remember is your peeing down the side of my motor-car... !'

A shocked silence was followed by explanations and gales of laughter on both sides!

When another great sportsman came to Lobb's, the tables were neatly turned, and it was Eric Lobb who was on the receiving end. The man was G. T. S. Stevens, perhaps the best schoolboy cricketer of all time. Stevens went on from school to play for Middlesex and England. He scored 466 not out in a house match at University College School, Hampstead, and played for the Gentlemen *versus* the Players while he was still there. (Just to prove he was human too, he did once drop Wilfred Rhodes three times off consecutive balls when fielding in the gully, having already dropped Jack Hobbs!)

His visit was another excuse for reminiscing, for his career and Eric Lobb's had overlapped at UCS, and they had at one time been neighbours in Alexandra Road. Stevens had a past grievance to bring up.

'Eric, do you remember reporting a burglary at our house in St John's Wood?'

'Well, yes, now you come to mention it ... I remember my brother and I were at home on our own and we saw a torch being used in your house. As we knew your family had not yet moved in, we called the police.'

'Yes. Thank you very much ... My girl-friend and I just managed to escape over the garden wall before they got in!'

In the 'sixties, one member of the Lobb staff was caught in the middle of a dispute between the manager and a customer. So he went into Eric Lobb's office and said, 'Excuse me, sir, but there's an elderly lady in the shop who's chosen some shoes but says she can only afford £7 for them.'

'Don't be ridiculous. This is a shop, not an Arab market. We don't barter. Tell her the price is the price and that's that.' The fitter withdrew to return two minutes later.

'I'm sorry sir, but she's very persistent. She says she's an old out-of-work actress, and can't afford any more than £7.'

'I can't help that, tell her to go away. Who is she anyway?' The fitter returned two minutes later.

'I'm very sorry, sir, but she won't go. She says her name is Ivy St Helier.'

'IVY ST HELIER? Why didn't you say so before? Tell her "Heigh Ho, If Love were all".'

'I couldn't say that, sir. I'd be embarrassed.'

'Go on, I insist.'

The fitter went off wearily to re-enter two minutes later.

'You'll have to come sir. She's in tears. You've really done it now.'

Eric Lobb went out into the shop to see the original Manon La Crevette from *Bitter Sweet*, a part which Noël Coward wrote especially for her. Though that was in 1929, she still looked marvellous and was visibly moved to be remembered.

'Miss St Helier, it's an honour to have you in our shop. Please have any pair you fancy with my compliments,' he said, much to the chagrin of the fitter who had been trying to fight the rearguard action.

Before she left with her new shoes there was an exchange of theatrical memories culminating in a memorable exit line as she left.

'Today they tell us to play it cool. *I* always played it hot!'

This abrupt change from hard-headed businessman to admiring benefactor is perhaps a useful clue to understanding the character of Eric Lobb. Although he can be firm, realistic, strong and resilient in adversity, there is underneath a kindness and generosity always ready to break through. As an employer, a harsh critic might suggest he was a paternalist, but that would be too cynical to be accurate. Rather, he is a man who genuinely likes his staff, admires their skill and is prepared to reward them for it, yet likes them to feel that theirs is more than just a business relationship with him.

Charlie Moore, John Lake and Ernest Sandford, the three men who worked for Lobb's for over sixty years, were given a slap-up luncheon at the Connaught in 1958, and all the staff have been given a Christmas Party, the annual

'Lwobble', for every one of the last twenty-five years. (In
the early years, every employee was supplied with a chicken
from the Lobb farming enterprise, but since the supply failed
in later years, Eric Lobb has gone out, bought the requisite
number himself and pretended they still came from the
same source.)

Gestures like these are so patently sincere that there is no
suggestion of an employer trying to show himself in a good
light, but rather of a man trying to retain some old-fashioned
courtesy in his relationships. Preserving the best from the
past is the policy which best characterises the firm today;
one may describe Lobb's as 'old-fashioned' in the finest
sense of the word. For over thirty years, the firm has been
built in one man's image, an image which many people
continue to find attractive, and one which should ensure
that Lobb's will continue to flourish and reap the rewards
for the ever more unique product they supply. If so, the
future should be bright indeed: some future historian may
find in the Lobb account books for the reign of King Charles
III such names as Lord David Frost, Sir Michael Jagger and
Countess Twiggy!

There is, however, one final anecdote, again a true one,
which shows that successful businessmen are as fallible as
the rest of us. The first time that Eric Lobb was called to visit
His Royal Highness the Duke of Edinburgh to measure him
for a new pair of boots, the 'phone rang just as he and
Charlie Moore were getting ready to go to Clarence House.
Eric was in the process of changing his own shoes but he
answered the call to be asked as the Duke had a pressing
engagement, whether the fitting could be taken immediately.
Eric and Charlie dashed into St James's Street, hailed a taxi
and jumped into it. It was then Charlie pointed out that for
the Royal Bootmaker to turn up wearing one brown shoe
and one black was not the best advertisement to present to a
Very Important Customer.

INDEX

Abrahams, Harold, 103
Agate, James, 106
Alexander, Sir George, 69, 70, 71, 76, 93
Alexandra, Queen, 46
Amies, Hardy, 138
Archer, William, 72
Arlen, Michael, 105-6
Arthur's Club, 60

Balanchine, George, 107
Barber, Noel, 2
Barber, Anthony, 138
Barrie, J. M., 71
Barrymore, Ethel, 72
Barrymore, John, 72
Battenburg, Prince Louis Alexander, 96
Beaton, Cecil, 105
Bedford, Duke of, 138
Beecham, Thomas, 94
Beerbohm, Max, 4, 76
Beery, Wallace, 106
Belgium, King Albert of, 96
Bennett, Arnold, 97
Benson, Frank, 69
Berenson, Bernard, 97
Blake, Sexton, 4, 5
Bloomfield, Robert, 15
Boodles Club, 60
Boot and Shoe Reporter, The, 53
Bootmakers (*see* Shoemakers),
Boucicault, Dion, 72, 94
Bradlaugh, Charles, 19
Brighton College, 89, 90, 109

British Museum, 14
Brooks, Thomas, 62, 63
Brummel, Beau, 30
Brunel, Marc, 51
Buchanan, Jack, 138
Burgess, Guy, 107
Byron, Lord, 30, 135, 136

Calf, waxed, 10, 11
Campbell, Mrs. Patrick, 70
Cape, Jonathan, 96, 102
Carey, William, 15
Carnegie, Andrew, 79
Carslake, Brownie, 96
Carstairs, John Paddy, 138
Caruso, Enrico, 94, 95
Castle, Vernon, 99
Cato Street Conspiracy, 19
Chaliapin, Feodor, 95
Chamberlain, Neville, 75, 102, 107
Charteris, Leslie, 105
Chase, Pauline, 94
Cheyney, Peter, 138
Chicago Exhibition (1893), 58
Churchill, Horace, 30
Churchill, Randolph, 107
Churchill, Winston, 126
Clarke, William, 52
Clore, Charles, 138
Cocoa Tree Club, 30, 60
Compton, Denis, 138
Conservative Club, 60
Conway, Sir Martin, 75
Cooch Behar, Maharajah, 74
Cordwainers College, 90

Craftsmen, 8-10
Craigie, Mrs., 69, 73
Creevey, 30
Culbertson, Ely, 105
Cunard family, 74
Cusack, Cyril, 138
Czinner, Paul, 106

D. H. Evans, 67
Dahl, Roald, 138
Daily Mail, The, 4
Darbangha, Maharajdharja, 106
Davenport, Allan, 19
Davenport, Walter Bromley, 107
Debenham and Freebody, 67
Dekker, Thomas, 17
de Delincourt, Martin 106
Delius, Frederic, 94
Despard, Colonel, 19
Devonshire Club, 60
Disney, Walt, 69
Disraeli Benjamin, 69
Docker, Bernard, 107
Donovan, 138
Douglas, Lord Alfred, 76, 79-80,
    135
Douglas, Justice William O., 132,
    133, 134
Du Maurier, Gerald, 104
Dvořák, Antonín, 69

Economist, The, 135
Edinburgh, Duke of, 3, 129, 142
Edward IV, 15
Edward VII, 2, 46, 59, 96
Edward VIII, 108
Edwardes, George, 71
Einzig, Paul, 105
Elizabeth II, 3, 129
Esquire magazine, 4
Esterhazy, Prince Louis, 74
Ethiopia, Emperor of, 3
Evans, Godfrey, 138
Eyre, Simon, 17-18

Firbank, Ronald, 97, 102
Fox, George, 15, 17
Franck, Cesar, 69
Frohmann, Charles, 71, 72

Galsworthy, John, 5
General Strike, the, 96, 101, 112-113
George V, 96, 108
George VI, 108
Gifford, William, 15
Gibbon, Edward, 30
Gibbs, Sir Philip, 5
Gilbert and Sullivan, 70
Gillray, James, 30
Gold rush, Australian, 35-37
Great Exhibitions (1851), 43
    (1862), 43-44
Greet, Ben, 71
Grossmith, George and Weedon,
    93
Gubb, Tommy, 139, 140

Hamilton, Gerald, 97
Hardy, Thomas, 19
Hargreaves, Edward Hammond,
    34, 35
Harris, Frank, 70, 76-78, 79
Harrods, 33
Hartnell, Norman, 103
Harty, Sir Hamilton, 106
Harvey, Laurence, 138
Hawtrey, Charles, 69, 70, 71
Henderson, Sir Neville, 107
Henson, Josiah, 65
Hepburn, Katherine, 138
Herbert, Thomas (clockmaker), 45
Hicks, Seymour, 70, 71
Hitler, Adolf, 107
Hoby, 'the Great', 30
Hochhuth, Rolf, 126
Hope-Boyce, Mr., 117
Hunt, Holman, 33
Hylton, Jack, 138

Illustrated Sporting and
    Dramatic News, 124
Inchiquin, Lord, 74
Industrial revolution, 51-52
International American
    Centennial Exhibition, 57
Iran, King of, 3
Irving, Henry, 70, 72
Irving, H. B., 71

Isherwood, Christopher, 97

Jaipur, Maharaja of, 106
Jardine, Douglas, 106
Johnson, Amy, 106
Jordan, King Hussein of, 138

Kent, Sherman, 120
Kipling, Rudyard, 69, 94
Kleinwort, Cyril, 107
Knoblock, Edward, 96, 102
Kulp, Benjamin, 130-132

Lake, John, 91, 108, 117, 141
Lamb, Lady Caroline, 136
Leather, 9
Leather workers, 8-10
Lewis, John, 67-68
Liebig family, 74
Lloyd George, 90
Lloyd Wright, Frank, 69
Lobb, Betsy, 83, 88-89, 91, 100, 101,
    114, 117, 134
Lobb, Caroline (née Caroline
    Richards), 39, 48, 49
Lobb, Caroline Victoria, 39, 62-63
Lobb, Eric, 84, 90, 108, 109-116,
    117, 118, 123-127, 128-133, 135
Lobb, Flora, 48
Lobb, Frederick, 48
Lobb, John, (founder), 2, 5, 24, 25,
    26-28, 29, 31-32, 34, 35-41, 42-
    43, 44, 46-50, 57-58, 60, 80, 87,
    91, 111, 125, 137
Lobb, John, (son of founder), 39,
    62, 63-64, 87
Lobb, John Hunter, 84
Lobb, John Hunter, (son of
    William Lobb), 134
Lobb, Mary Aline, 39, 62
Lobb, Victor, 84, 101-102
Lobb, William, 84, 90-91, 102, 108,
    115, 117, 134
Lobb, William Hunter, 48, 62, 64-
    65, 68, 70-74, 76, 80-82, 83-87,
    88, 91, 101, 129
Lobb and Hampley, 46
Lohr, Marie, 94

London and Provincial Union of
    Hand-Sewn Boot and Shoe-
    makers, 81
Lubomirski, Prince Stanislaus, 74
Lucas, E. V., 103
Lugosi, Bela, 106

McCormack, 'Count' John, 95, 102
MacKay, Ruth, 94
Mackenzie, Compton, 103
Macmillan, Harold, 138
Macrae, Duncan, 94
Madox Brown, Ford, 33-34
Madrid, Prince of Asturias from,
    74
Madras, Rajah Pudiekoto of, 74
Magnus, Sir Philip, 46
Maples, 67
Marconi, Guglielmo, 103-104
Mason, A. E. W., 97
Massey, Raymond, 104
Massine, Leonide, 107
Master Bootmakers' Association,
    128
Matthews, A. E., 93, 102
Maugham, Somerset, 105
Mayhew, Henry, 19-24
Menjou, Adolphe, 104
Moore, Charlie, 93, 116, 124-125,
    141, 142
Moore, Thomas, 68, 91, 93, 102,
    108, 115-116, 119
Morgan, Charles, 4
Morning Post, The, 20

Nast, Condé, 96
Neilson, Julia, 69
Neilson-Terry, Phyllis, 94
New University Club, 60
Northampton shoe factories, 11, 19,
    23
Northcote, Henry Stafford, 75

Oliver's shoe stores, 66
Olympics, Paris, 103
Oppenheimer, Bernard, 98
Orpen, Sir William Newenham
    Montagu, 98, 102

O'Toole, Peter, 138

Page, Handley, 103
Pallister, Admiral, 75
Panama Canal Company, 75
Paris Exhibitions, (1867) 57, (1878) 57, (1889) 57, (1900 and 1937) 59
Pataudi, Nawab of, 107
Peck, Gregory, 138
Pendrill, Charles, 19
'Percentage' System, 59-60
Philological School, Marylebone, 64
Phillips, Admiral Sir John, 126
Phillips, Stephen, 69
Pinero, Arthur, 93
Pope, Alexander, 30
Porter, Cole, 98, 102
Preston, Thomas, 19
Prince of Wales, (ship), 126
Pulitzer, Joseph, 74-75
Punch magazine, 135

Rachmaninov, Sergei, 69
Radcliffe, William, 126-127
Randolph, D. M., 51
Rathbone, Basil, 103
Repulse, (ship), 126
Reventlow, Count, 74
Referee, The (sporting and literary paper), 72-74
Richards, Caroline (see Lobb, Caroline)
Richards, Frederick, 39-40, 46, 49, 60-61, 65, 68, 91
Richards, Thomas, 39
Robertson, Tom, 70
Robinson, Edward G., 127
Robinson, Peter, 48, 67
Ross, Robert, 76
Rossetti, Dante Gabriel, 33
Rothschilds, 74
Rowntree, Seebohm, 78
Royal Warrants, 45, 129

Sachs, Hans, 16, 17
St. Crispin, 14-15, 16
St. Hugh, 15, 18

St. Helier, Ivy, 141
St. James's Street, 4, 8, 12, 30
Sandford, Ernest, 91, 141
Saunders, Jim, 54, 91-92, 124
Sayaji Rao III, His Highness Maharajah Gaekwar Baroda Sir, 99
Schroeder, Baron Paul, 107
Shaw, George Bernard, 69, 72, 94
Sherbourne, Lord, 74
Shinwell, Emmanuel, 129
Shoemakers' Holiday, The, 17-18, 138
Shoemaking, 8-10, 21, 23, 46, 51-52, 53, 54-55
Sikorski, General, 126
Sinatra, Frank, 138
Singer Company of America, 51-52
Smerdon, Betsy, (see Lobb, Betsy)
Smyth, Ethel, 94
Spa Fields demonstration (1816), 19
Speight, Robert, 5
Stein, Gertrude, 8
Stevens, G. T., 140
Stone, Frank, 97
Stone, Marcus, 97-98
Strauss, Johann, 94
Sullivan (see Gilbert and Sullivan)
Swinnerton, Frank, 97, 102
Sunday Times, The, 135
Sydney Morning Herald, The, 35

Tankerville, Lord, 74
Tearle, Godfrey, 94
Tempest, Marie, 69
Tennent, H. M., 99
Tenniel, Sir John, 69
Terris, Ellaline, 70, 71
Thailand, King of, 2
Thatched House Club, 60
Thomas's, (bootmakers), 31, 39, 60
Times, The, 35
Timpson, William, 66
Tree, Beerbohm, 69

United Eton and Harrow Club, 60

University College School, Hampstead, 90

Verdi, Guiseppe, 69
Verulam Club, 60
Vienna Exhibition, (1873), 57

Wace, Robert, 127
Wagner, Richard, 16
Walpole, Hugh, 105
Warburton, Colonel Sir Robert, 75
Waterlow, Sir Sydney, 75
War, First World, 88-89, 91-92
War, Second World, 120-123

Welles, Orson, 138
Wellington, Duke of, 30
West End Makers and Closers, 54-55
Wheatley, Dennis, 106
Webb, Clifton, 103
Whiteley's William, 85, 86
White's coffee house, 30-31, 60
Whitney, William Collins, 75
Wilde, Oscar, 76
Wilshin, Leonard, 63
Woolner, Thomas, 33

Yale University, 120